MICHIGAN
- VS -
EVERYBODY

Inside the **WOLVERINES'** 2023
NATIONAL CHAMPIONSHIP Season

Angelique Chengelis

TRIUMPH
BOOKS

Library of Congress Cataloging-in-Publication Data
available upon request

This book is available in quantity at special discounts for your group
or organization. For further information, contact:

Triumph Books LLC
814 North Franklin Street
Chicago, Illinois 60610
(312) 337-0747
www.triumphbooks.com

Printed in U.S.A.
ISBN: 978-1-63727-691-4

Editorial production and design by Alex Lubertozzi
All photos courtesy of AP Images unless otherwise indicated

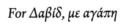

For Δαβίδ, με αγάπη

– CONTENTS –

– FOREWORD –
by
JAKE BUTT

EVERY YEAR in college football, a champion is crowned. Certainly, each team and its fan base feels it's special and memorable. Of course, all champions are special in their own right, but every now and then, we witness something truly special. Something we haven't seen before and may never see again, especially considering the broader landscape of college football.

Rarely do we remember the times everything went according to plan. In fact, there is no great story without great challenge and adversity. The great warriors and teams aren't idolized because they had it easy. The greatest among us are remembered for what we had to endure, overcome, and persevere.

True adversity creates a split in time, a fork in the road. Suddenly, when facing great challenge, two paths appear in front of us. Will we be divided? Will we crumble and seek comfort? Will we do what's easy and reassuring? Or will we choose the other path? The path that takes the very pressure that crumbles others and uses that pressure to bring us closer together. The path that requires absolute unity and alignment, where at every corner, players, coaches, and staff choose to stand by one another. The path where challenging questions have to be answered and addressed seemingly with no end in sight.

In the ever-changing world of college football, will we ever see a team like the 2023 Wolverines again?

The roster was full of leaders and men the Michigan community got to follow and watch grow up in the Big House: Mikey Sainristil, the definition of a Michigan Man, a talented wide receiver who was asked to switch to nickelback to help shore up the team's secondary. When asked by coach Jim Harbaugh if he was willing to move to defense, he said, "Whatever you need, Coach." Blake Corum, the heartbeat of the Michigan offense. I will never forget the 2022 Michigan–Ohio State game, being down on the field for warm-ups in Columbus and watching tears roll down Corum's face as he searched deeply for the ability to help the team win. A week prior, in the midst of a Heisman campaign, Corum endured a significant knee injury in the second quarter against Illinois, ending his season and a chance at the prestigious award. J.J. McCarthy, a future NFL first-round pick at quarterback, who somehow saw into the future when tweeting to the Michigan fan base after a challenging stretch of tough losses in 2020, reminding them to breathe, have faith, and remember that every coach, player, and employee was doing everything they could to ensure the success of the program.

Of course, the list of impactful players and men could go on, but they were all led by their head coach, Jim Harbaugh. As a player, Harbaugh made a promise that he would lead his team to victory over Ohio State. In his introductory presser as Michigan head coach in 2015, he made no such promises. He only pledged excellence and effort. As one of the men who played for him, I can tell you wholeheartedly, he delivered on that promise. There is only one speed for Jim Harbaugh, full speed, but after years of trying, coming close, and ultimately falling short, it was time for Coach to renew his promises.

In a sense, 2023 felt like destiny. How could it not be destiny? When you consider the organic challenges that all teams face on the field in season and combine that with the outside challenges the team faced, there were countless opportunities to slip up and fail, but they didn't. Opening the season in their first three games with Harbaugh suspended only showed their character and resolve as a team. Quickly, it became clear this team was on a path to compete for another playoff berth and national title. The final three games of the season, starting with Penn State, would be the ultimate test. Of course, no one could've predicted they once again would be without their head coach, as Harbaugh was suspended for Michigan's responsibility in the alleged sign-stealing activity by Connor Stalions.

This book will cover everything that unfolded with Connor Stalions, but what won't be forgotten is the way the players carried themselves in those final three games—going on the road against an elite Penn State defense without their head coach and running the ball 32 straight times to secure a gritty victory. Surviving a trap game versus a dangerous Maryland team that gave OSU all they could handle earlier in the season. And of course, The Game.

There was a moment in the Ohio State game that I think is a microcosm of this team's identity. Every year The Game proves itself as one of the great rivalries in all of sport. But, in a matchup with over a century of deep and wide-reaching history, the 2023 matchup will be one that stands all by itself for many reasons: the great matchup of Ohio State receiver Marvin Harrison Jr. versus Michigan cornerback Will Johnson; Michigan's offensive line versus an improved Buckeye front seven; Blake Corum back and fully healthy. But there was one moment that will always stand out to me—a moment that, once again, highlights the unity of the program, the fan base, and the mission this team was on.

In the second half of the game, star offensive lineman, team captain, and veteran leader Zak Zinter went down, and things did not look good. We quickly heard from the broadcast that this was a serious injury, and he would need to be carted off. Anyone watching could feel the energy in the stadium—110,000 fans on both sides, dead quiet. The TV broadcast panned from player to player, showing battle-tested warriors with tears in their eyes. Sadness and concern set in and radiated throughout the stadium.

We don't know where it started, but somewhere in the stadium, a chant started to emerge. It was picked up and echoed continually until the entire stadium was chanting as one, "Let's go, Zak! Let's go, Zak!"

Alchemy was a medieval science and philosophy, in which the aim was the transmutation of base metals into gold. I've heard *alchemy* used to describe emotions as well. What we witnessed was the charged emotion of sadness and pain transmuted into unifying love and support. Clearly it energized the players, because on the very next play—the icing on the cake, which again, highlighted the unique character of this team—Blake Corum took a handoff 22 yards into the end zone. The crowd went absolutely nuts as Blake chose to celebrate by holding up six and then five fingers as a nod to his injured teammate's jersey No. 65.

Michigan would go on to beat Ohio State, finishing the regular season undefeated. The Wolverines would defeat Iowa to secure their third straight Big Ten championship. All eyes would now be on the College Football Playoff, where Michigan learned they would be back in the Rose Bowl against the powerhouse Alabama Crimson Tide.

We would get to see a match-up between Jim Harbaugh and Nick Saban, and would later find out it was Saban's last game as a head coach. Of course, Harbaugh left after the season for the NFL. Two great coaches meeting in a historic venue in the twilight of their tenures as heads of their respective programs. Destiny.

After the win over Alabama, it would be a match-up of the last Pac-12 champion, the Washington Huskies, and Michigan. Both rosters were littered with NFL talent, but even then, Michigan proved to be too much.

Michigan ran counter to conventional wisdom on how to build a successful team. Conventional wisdom said high-powered passing attack, bring in a ton of five-star recruits, that you needed to be the biggest spender to win at the highest level. While all those traits hold some truth and will always be important to a team's success, it was evident to anyone who watched that Michigan Wolverines team that they were playing for something much bigger. As the college football landscape continues to evolve, as we embrace the pay-for-play model and work toward the end of "amateurism," I believe it's fair to ask, will the '23 Wolverines be the last "classic" national champions?

In time, the finer details will fade. New champions will be crowned. Michigan will experience many more successes and challenges, but what makes the 2023 season so special is no one that was a part of that journey will ever forget how that team made them feel.

Jake Butt
Big Ten Network color analyst
2016 Michigan captain

"MICHIGAN vs. EVERYBODY"

THERE have been bold guarantees made before by players the week of a game, but this was gutsy.

A national championship. The Michigan football team would win a national championship. That's what returning running back Blake Corum declared during halftime of a basketball game on campus months before the start of the 2023 season. This wasn't his head coach, Jim Harbaugh, who as quarterback for the Wolverines in 1986, declared they would beat archrival Ohio State in Columbus.

"We're going to play in the Rose Bowl this year, I guarantee it," Harbaugh famously told reporters without prompting. "We'll beat Ohio State; we'll be in Pasadena on January 1."

That was big, no doubt, and became a part of Michigan–Ohio State lore as the Wolverines went on to back up their quarterback's words. But what Corum told the crowd that night on February 8, 2023, when the football team was being honored at midcourt for winning a second straight Big Ten championship, was enormous. This was a team that six weeks earlier had suffered its second consecutive loss in the College Football Playoff (CFP) semifinals. But Corum, a couple months removed from knee surgery, was brimming with confidence.

Maybe no one else knew exactly what Michigan could be in 2023, but he knew. With so many veterans choosing to skip the NFL to return to play another season for the Wolverines, starting with him, and including defensive back Mike Sainristil, linebacker Michael Barrett, receiver Cornelius Johnson, and offensive linemen Trevor Keegan and Zak Zinter, Corum knew.

"Man, it feels good to be back!" Corum, standing with the microphone at midcourt, told the appreciative Crisler Center crowd while some of his teammates tossed T-shirts to fans. "And I don't have much to say. All I've gotta say is, we're gonna run it back. We're gonna win the national championship and go down in history. That's all I got. Go Blue!"

The Michigan players there didn't seem remotely shocked. Corum returned the microphone, offensive lineman Trevor Keegan clapped at the conclusion of his comments, and they all walked back toward the tunnel, fist-bumping a few kids and arena workers on their way out. It was as though Corum had not said something unexpected or out of the ordinary. He said what they all believed.

That Corum's guarantee didn't gain more traction nationally was a bit stunning. There were some around the country who shrugged it off as merely big talk from a team that couldn't get past the CFP semifinals the last two years, first losing to eventual national champion Georgia in 2021 and then to TCU in 2022. The perception seemed to be that as long as the Bulldogs were around, Michigan could make all the bold predictions it wanted, but Georgia, which had won the national title in 2022 as well, was king.

"We have a team that is very special right now," Corum said at Big Ten media days in late July, not long before the start of preseason camp. "A lot of guys coming back, [quarterback] J.J. [McCarthy] has another year under his belt, we have transfers—Drake Nugent, LD [LaDarius Henderson], big [Myles] Hinton. Up front, we're great. Team-wise, we're great. We've been working our butts off this summer, and I believe in my guys. I believe in the camaraderie, the brotherly love that we have within each other right now, it's crazy.

"What I'm telling the guys now is that it's just day to day now. We've had enough dreaming, we've had enough talk about the national championship, now it's just day to day. We have to beat ECU first, we can't think too far ahead. Be where our feet are. We have to take care of the regular-season schedule, beat our rivals, and then, if we get there, we've just got to get over the hump. For me, I have high standards, so yeah, it's win or bust. I think the guys know that, but we don't have to say anything, we know what it is."

There was no way Corum could possibly have known the twists and turns that awaited the Wolverines as they ventured on their journey to attempt to fulfill his guarantee. But he never wavered. They never worried. Even when not one, but two NCAA investigations ultimately sidelined their head coach for six regular-season games and put Michigan in the national headlines for everything other than their winning, they remained unfazed. The Wolverines would be called cheaters and their coach a liar, but the players shut out the noise and rallied behind a new motto, "Michigan vs. Everybody." It was once a cute slogan sold on sweatshirts and T-shirts to increase players' name, image, likeness (NIL) income, but it became the Wolverines' identity and bolstered Corum's faith in his guarantee.

Michigan's Rose Bowl College Football Playoff semifinal against Alabama on New Year's Day was the hurdle the Wolverines finally had to clear to play for a national title. The Wolverines were 0–2 in semifinal games, and the Crimson Tide had been among the four semifinalists eight times since the inception of the CFP in 2014. They had more appearances than any team and had won three national titles in that span.

Again, Corum felt secure in his promise made so many months earlier. And with Michigan as the No. 1 seed, he believed it even more.

"I don't really care what people say at the end of the day," he said before the Rose Bowl. "For me, I try to stand on what I say, and I'm pretty good at it. I did say before the season, it's a championship-or-bust-type of season, so I'm going to stand on that and do everything in my power to make sure this team is ready to take the field and play Alabama. Everyone is able to have their own opinions, but for me what I said before the season, I still stand on it. It is championship or bust."

Eleven months after Corum made his guarantee on the Crisler Center floor, he was back again with his teammates and coaches on January 13, 2024, to celebrate what he promised they would achieve—a national championship. He wore a shirt with one of his new catchphrases—BUSINESS IS FINISHED—as he stepped to the arena microphone with teammates and coaches before and around him. It felt a bit like déjà vu as his February comments were replayed on the videoboard above. Corum smiled.

"I promised y'all," he said after the video ended. "And what did we do?"

He didn't think the team could get any closer because it had always been so tight-knit. But through the adversity of the season, the players found a way to insulate themselves from outside noise and remain undeterred, as Corum explained:

> We didn't let the outside sources, outside people bother us. We didn't let anyone change our thoughts or what we thought about ourselves or about this team. We just kept pushing, man.

When adversity hits, you can do two things: you can crumble, or you can keep going. We just kept going. We knew there was going to be a light at the end of the tunnel, and we didn't let anyone bother us. We knew our mission, and we knew we had to complete the mission. That's how we kind of attacked the season with everything that's happened.

A team together, everyone accomplishes more. That's what made us great. It's not one coach. It's not one captain. It's not one player. It's all of us coming together, and we all bought into. All right, this is our mindset, this is how we're going to attack each and every day, this is how we're going to stick together and just fight for other brothers.

Ultimately, a slogan became reality. For the players, it really did become Michigan vs. Everybody.

– 1 –

THE ROOTS OF
THE TITLE TEAM

EVERYONE remembers the ending, especially when celebratory maize and blue confetti spills from above as the most cherished trophy in college football is raised high. An overwhelming sense of euphoria is shared between players, coaches, and fans. Everyone remembers the welcome home and the cheers and the "one more year" chants directed at star players weighing their futures. And everyone remembers the parade and the thousands who braved cold, windy weather to witness a fun-loving, bare-chested offensive lineman with a crystal football in one hand and a beer in another. And everyone remembers the sold-out celebration and the speeches and the realization that this magical team would be together for this one last night.

Reaching the pinnacle of any pursuit and the joy that follows can be captured in photographs, videos, and in print with big, bold headlines. That's the championship moment embraced by all. It is a feeling easily shared by those who accomplished the feat and also by the family, friends, and fans who cheered for them along the way. Parents shed tears of pure joy for their child and his teammates upon accomplishing their most significant goal, and right next to them a fan who might have no personal connection to the players also sheds tears of pure joy because of the university love they share.

Michigan went undefeated through 15 games in 2023, including a victory over Washington in the title game to claim the national championship. All of that is tangible and real and a source of pride for so many. What is more challenging to understand and grasp is how exactly the Wolverines got there. Sure, they never lost a game, but that only explains a small part of the journey that undoubtedly had roots in the previous three seasons.

An achievement like this requires grit and focus, and that's in a *normal* year.

There was nothing, however, typical about this season for the Wolverines. The players had to dig deep and hold the team together amid controversy and allegations, but the thing is, the leaders on the team, the elder statesmen, had experienced rock bottom with the program. They had also lost in two previous CFP semifinal games. So when it came to dealing with the unpredictability off the field that affected the program and would ultimately keep their coach, Jim Harbaugh, from being on the sideline for six regular-season games, they knew how to respond and what buttons to push. Allegations, investigations, and controversy were as much a part of the season as touchdowns, stingy defense, and wins. But, in the end, the team was defined by its leaders, who never wavered in the face of these many challenges. The players never second-guessed, and they never allowed their goals to be derailed.

"When they doubted, when they disrespected, when they called us names—they said we were cheaters and said we didn't deserve what we had—none of that mattered to us," two-time captain Mike Sainristil said at that final celebration. "We stayed focused, kept our heads on straight, and week to week, we gave spankings out."

Michigan entered the season with an NCAA investigation that dated back to 2021 hanging over the program. Harbaugh faced a Level I violation, the most serious, for allegedly lying to and misleading investigators regarding impermissible recruiting during the COVID-19 recruiting dead period and would serve a three-game, school-imposed suspension at the start of the season. Another NCAA investigation involving allegations of an illegal scouting and sign-stealing scheme emerged just beyond the midway point of the season and would take drama to a new level around the program. Harbaugh was suspended the final three regular-season games by the Big Ten.

The "Michigan vs. Everybody" slogan, which had been sold on sweatshirts and T-shirts the last few years to generate name, image, likeness income, became an identity for the players and a rallying cry.

This gumption, this confidence, and general sense of ease among the players was the gift of the older players, the leaders on this team. There were other layers to the team's ability to operate with blinders, as well. Without question, quarterback J.J. McCarthy ruminating about the loss to TCU in the Fiesta Bowl CFP semifinal that ended the Wolverines' 2022 season was a big part of his drive entering his junior season. He had thrown two pick-sixes in a game in which Michigan was favored. The Wolverines fell short in their comeback, and he was determined to lead Michigan to glory in 2023. There also was Corum's very public promise of a national championship and, during the season, his frequent references to late NBA star Kobe Bryant, who during the 2009 NBA Finals famously said, "Job's not finished," even though the Lakers had gone ahead 2–0. This was his way of keeping his teammates from looking too far ahead.

To understand the success of the 2023 season is to understand the lessons learned from the dreadful 2–4 COVID-shortened season. The veterans, the core group of leaders on this '23 team held onto the feeling of that embarrassing season and never let it go—not in an unhealthy way, not even close. It was always a reference point, a way to measure growth. They knew what rock bottom felt like.

Former Michigan receiver Ronnie Bell thought back to that 2–4 season after winning the Wolverines' second-straight Big Ten championship in 2022 and described it perfectly. "Oh, man," he told reporters, "2020 was dark."

The Wolverines bottomed out on October 31, 2020, when they lost to rebuilding Michigan State 27–24. Then again, a week later they lost 38–21 at Indiana to snap a 24-game winning streak in that series. Then they lost the following week to Wisconsin. The 49–11 loss to the Badgers on November 14 was the Wolverines' worst home defeat in 85 years. Kirk Herbstreit seemed speechless on the ABC broadcast as he said, "I can't believe this is happening."

It was McCarthy, a five-star quarterback recruit committed to Michigan but not yet on the team, who surfaced on social media to attempt to calm the fan base during that dreadful 2020 season. In a series of posts on Twitter on November 15, 2020, McCarthy wrote that there's always a "light at the end of the tunnel" and that "support is the only thing that they need right now," encouraging fans to keep the faith.

"I want all Michigan fans to do this. Take 3 deep breaths...And have faith," McCarthy wrote. "Faith that every single coach, player, employee in that building is doing everything they possibly can to be great."

McCarthy was on to something, but it was too soon to realize.

The Wolverines would cancel its final three games because of a COVID-19 outbreak. That's when there was a groundswell of support to move on from head coach Jim Harbaugh. Instead, athletics director Warde Manuel retained Harbaugh on Manuel's terms, slashing his pay in half but giving him a heavily incentivized new contract.

For Harbaugh and Michigan, the 2020 season represented a realization that plenty needed to change heading into 2021. That January he signed a new four-year contract extension and also overhauled his staff. He moved on from defensive coordinator Don Brown and replaced him with Mike Macdonald, who had been with the Baltimore Ravens. Ravens head coach John Harbaugh recommended Macdonald to his younger brother as a solution to spark the defense. The staff got younger and included Mike Hart, Michigan's all-time leading rusher, and former Michigan receiver Ron Bellamy, while defensive backs coach Steve Clinkscale was an instant hit with players who said they were able to relate to him and his style.

The players, though, also knew they had to make changes.

"You're supposed to have that Michigan standard," edge rusher Aidan Hutchinson, who would become an All-American as well as a Heisman Trophy runner-up in 2021, said after a Detroit Lions practice in 2023. "I was hell-bent, everyone on that team was hell-bent on turning things around. I felt our senior year, new coaches, everything aligned. The people who were the leaders were in the right place, and the coaches were in the right place."

The flip switched after the COVID season for the Wolverines. Players left, new coaches came in, and the team was finding its balance.

"We just had a lot of selfish players, didn't really have a good culture," Keegan said of the 2020 season when discussing how it changed the program. "There were people who were here to go to the NFL, and that was all they cared about. Now, there's dudes who have created a brotherhood, who care for each other, want to come in here every day and work, achieve goals together. It's completely different."

Linebacker Michael Barrett, like Keegan, witnessed and lived through that rock-bottom season. He was a freshman in 2018 and had worked his way up to a full-time starter in 2020. With Brown's departure, Barrett, who had been plugged into a very specific Viper position in that defensive scheme, wasn't sure what this meant for him. He never sulked and he didn't consider transferring. Instead, he stayed, made himself invaluable on special teams in 2021, and then returned to a starting role at linebacker in 2022.

"Everybody who stayed, we just made that pact that we'd never feel that way again," Barrett said, recalling the shift following the 2020 season. "We knew what we could do, the kind of team that we could have. And we just went up from there."

Barrett had a similar feeling to Trevor Keegan, that there were too many players focused on themselves and concerned with individual accomplishments. A change in that attitude was part of the culture shift at Michigan.

"What's good for the hive is good for the bee," Barrett said. "Everybody's kinda working for the person next to them. Everybody wants to see their brother succeed. There's no bad looks from anybody or anything like that. It's more of a family. It's a little tighter than it was in previous years."

Harbaugh changed his approach too. When he appeared at Big Ten media days in 2021, he made his renewed mission and vision clear. And for a change of pace, he spoke openly about the need to beat archrival Ohio State.

"Well, I'm here before you, enthusiastic and excited as I ever am, always am, even more to have at it, to win the championship, to beat Ohio [State] and our rival Michigan State," Harbaugh said. "That's what we want to do, and we're going to do it or die trying."

Harbaugh was beaming and said it with such conviction—as if he were willing it to be true just by saying it out loud. And maybe that's what the program needed coming out of the darkness of 2020. It needed the public to know things were changing, attitudes had been shifted, and the Wolverines were going to die trying to make a difference in the program's culture that would set a foundation for future teams. And that's what Michigan did in 2021 with Cade McNamara at quarterback, finally beating Ohio State after losing eight straight and going on to win the program's first Big Ten title since 2004.

McCarthy, the recruit who in 2020 had told the fan base to relax, said things were going to change and had his opportunity in 2022, winning the starting job after Game 2. He had stood with fellow freshmen, including running back Donovan Edwards, after losing in the College Football Playoff semifinal to Georgia and watched the Bulldogs' celebration. It was the first time the Wolverines had made the final four, and McCarthy wanted to soak it all in. He studied it.

A year later, the Wolverines were favored but lost to TCU in the semifinal. McCarthy answered a question at the news conference and abruptly got up and walked off. Edwards and Sainristil, who sat at the postgame podium with McCarthy, were supposed to also leave with him in a coordinated move, but they remained as McCarthy walked off.

"We'll be back, I promise that," McCarthy said before leaving the podium.

He wanted his early departure from the news conference to make a statement.

"Just that we're ready to get right to work," he said. "It wasn't anything against the media or saying I don't want to answer questions, I'm too mad. It was just I wanted to be in the locker room with my guys, all the seniors I'm never going to see again, and just be there to relish in those last moments with them."

But it was more than that. McCarthy has always been a student of motivational speaking and read countless books about successful athletes and their paths to success. He knew that Michigan could build off that second semifinal loss. He hadn't experienced the 2020 season as a player, but he had soaked in the pain of another CFP loss and stood on the field again watching another team celebrate. Having a quarterback who understood what it would take to get over that barrier and make a national title game along with leaders who were molded in many ways and endured the COVID season, it seemed like an unbeatable combination.

"Everything that we went through, it forged us," McCarthy said before the 2023 season. "Motivated us in the off-season to be better, do the extra rep, do more. I feel like it is ultimately the pain and failure that pushes you over the hump, pushes you to limits you've never been. When you lose a game like that, especially in the fashion that we lost, that feeling just doesn't go away after you lose that game. It's ultimately one of the best things that ever happened to me, and I'm extremely grateful for it. It changed my ultimate mindset and drive."

About six weeks before the start of the season, there was a brightness in Harbaugh's outlook as he and the team drew closer to the start of 2023. Maybe that was to be expected considering the Wolverines were coming off back-to-back Big Ten championships and CFP appearances, and returned a number of starters who could have departed for the NFL. And, of course, McCarthy was returning for a second full season as starting quarterback. This was the most talented team he ever had at Michigan, and it was clear Harbaugh loved the chemistry and makeup of this group.

"I was really surprised after the '21 season," Harbaugh recalled prior to the 2023 season. "You felt like, 'Okay, this is as good as it can get with everybody, players, coaches, staff going in the same direction.' In '22, there was that cultural momentum that seemed even better. Now, I'm kind of saying it to myself, 'It's gotta be as good as it can get.' Seeing our players, our staff, our coaches, seems like there's even more cultural momentum. It's been fun to be around."

The team took a spring trip to New York and Washington, D.C., with a few other stops along the way, and the bonds among teammates were deepened.

"Everybody seems to be in a good place," Harbaugh said. "They seem regrouped and refreshed. I think the time off was good for them."

There were a number of things that made the Wolverines a Big Ten favorite. Having McCarthy back was key. Harbaugh had a special relationship with his quarterback and vice versa. With Harbaugh having played quarterback at Michigan and during a long NFL career, they spoke the same language. Harbaugh admired McCarthy for always putting the team first.

"I look at the great quarterbacks like Josh Allen and Patrick Mahomes—I'm not with them every day, but you can just tell by looking at how they play the game and what they say, especially about their teammates, there's a willingness there to do," Harbaugh said. "That's the secret sauce in a quarterback. You could have all the different attributes which Patrick Mahomes and Josh Allen do, and so does J.J. They also got that willingness to do anything for their teammates. Because of that, their teammates and their coaches, like me, would follow him anywhere. I would recommend that anyone on the team would follow J.J anywhere that he's leading."

It was also the return of players like Corum, in the Heisman Trophy running until he suffered a knee injury in the 11th game of the regular season in 2022; and offensive line starters Zak Zinter and Keegan; not to mention Sainristil, Barrett, and Cornelius Johnson. Their returns were impactful in terms of what Harbaugh referred to as that "cultural momentum." Harbaugh had told Corum to head to the NFL. Corum decided he wanted a full off-season to train and prepare and get back to his best football while leading the Wolverines. When Corum told his head coach he'd be back, Harbaugh laughed and said he'd support that decision, knowing full well what having his presence would mean, not just for the run game but for the team as a whole.

"When you know him, it clicks immediately. That's who he is," Harbaugh said. "He's been a guy that's knocking on the door of the weight room at 6:00 in the morning. We can't let you in till 6:00. He's maniacal in his preparation and his training, he's just on everything and every detail. I think [returning] really gave him an opportunity to take his time and to get right. He's one of those guys, in terms of character and who he is as a teammate, it's up there with the elites. The greats. It's awesome."

Initially, it was about building a winning culture at Michigan. That's what 2021 was about, building that foundation, laying brick after brick. Then the 2022 season built it even more with a win at Ohio State, the first for Michigan since 2000. It was a major accomplishment. With the returns of Corum and the veterans, it was about sustaining the culture and also adding to it.

"They came back because they love Michigan," Michigan offensive coordinator/offensive line coach Sherrone Moore said in the off-season. "They've got a goal as a team to be great."

There was nothing, it seemed, that concerned Harbaugh about this team.

"It's truly amazing—we don't have any bad guys," Harbaugh said. "There's no bad person [among the] players, coaches, or staff—especially the players.... There's elite, great guys; there's guys that are good guys that are learning from the other guys. You've got the Heisman-habits guys, the great guys. No bad guys. Either that or they're impeccable with their timing, because every time I look at them, they're doing right. Every time I check the class attendance, they're do-right guys. Our guys have watched the Hassan Haskins come through, Aidan Hutchinson, evaluated them, emulated them, and try to go make them proud. See that with Blake Corum. Just get in Blake Corum's pocket, do what he does. So many guys like that. There's momentum there. There's a real cultural momentum taking place."

Harbaugh's good humor wasn't just about his players and coaches. It was generated, in part, by the feeling he'd get every time he'd be in the building. He sensed an energy that was hard to describe, but he loved it, and Harbaugh gave plenty of credit for the culture development to the director of the strength program, Ben Herbert.

"The weight room, it's the best. Coach Herb and his staff, I love going down there," Harbaugh said. "Something new. He's going to tell me something that the staff has come up with. Try this piece of equipment. They'll show me what it is. Just an unbelievable energy there, the center of player development. Fun place to be. I enjoy the heck out of it every day."

It was hard to imagine, based on Harbaugh's sunny demeanor, that a few years earlier, there was little to enjoy about the Michigan football program.

Michigan's potential for success heading into 2023 wasn't entirely a result of how the program responded to the 2020 season, but it would be foolish to think that brutal season had nothing to do with the progress and success the Wolverines had started to experience. For the veteran players, the ones who had experienced that low point, it certainly was something that fueled their resolve. They knew where Michigan had come from, and it motivated them to know it was up to them to keep that alive. Maybe the freshmen couldn't relate, but because the leaders of the team knew how they never wanted to feel again, they could apply what they had learned and how they dealt with it to any sort of adversity on the field—and, they'd discover, to deal with off-the-field issues.

"The mindset has been there since after COVID, because that's when we got counted out as a program," Sainristil said. "It was like, all right, that's how everybody feels about us—let's go prove them wrong."

And that's how the Wolverines headed into the 2023 season: a bit of a chip on their shoulder despite two seasons of success, but always reminding themselves that 2020 wasn't that long ago.

– 2 –

NOT "JUST ABOUT
A CHEESEBURGER"

BIG TEN media days in late July are a time for all of the conference coaches to share their thoughts on the upcoming season, what their rosters look like, and who might stand out. They field questions about anything and everything. Everyone is usually in a good mood antici-pating the start of another college football season, and coaches exude plenty of confidence in their teams and their chances. Harbaugh was always a big draw at the event the day Michigan appeared. As coach of the two-time defending Big Ten champions, there was no doubt he would have an even bigger media contingent surrounding him during his one-hour interview session.

That would be the case no matter what. But a day before the event in Indianapolis and two days before Harbaugh would speak to the media, news broke that Michigan and the NCAA were finalizing a negotiated resolution that would result in a four-game suspension for Harbaugh and one-game suspensions for assistants Sherrone Moore and Grant Newsome for committing NCAA violations stemming from alleged violations during the 2021 COVID-19 recruiting dead period. Michigan had received a draft of a Notice of Allegations from the NCAA in January that detailed the Level II violations, including impermissible recruiting visits, but also levied a Level I, the NCAA's harshest, against Harbaugh for allegedly lying to and misleading investigators.

Michigan officials were convinced this news was strategically leaked by the NCAA before the Big Ten media days where Harbaugh would address the media as a way to embarrass him. He took the stage two days after the negotiated resolution was reported and was almost immediately asked about the four-game suspension, which would mean Harbaugh missing the three nonconference games and the Big Ten opener against Rutgers.

"As you probably already know, I'm not allowed to talk about any aspect of that ongoing situation," Harbaugh, standing at the podium, told the crowd of reporters. "I'm with you—I'd love to lay it all out there. Nothing to be ashamed of, but now is not that time. That's about all there is to say about that."

The players who represented Michigan at media days, including Blake Corum and Mike Sainristil, predicted the team would rally around Harbaugh in his absence from the sideline those first four games. "If anything, it's going to make us go even harder," Corum said. "We're going to do this for Coach Harbaugh, if that's the case."

Sainristil said that although the players had not spent much time discussing the possibility that Harbaugh might be suspended, they would respond maturely. "I know what he'd want us to do is go out there and play a great brand of football and lead on for the Block M and play Michigan football. Play fast, play hard, play physical," Sainristil said. "Do what it is that he prepares us to do. Whether he's with us or not, we're going to play as if he was right there coaching us."

But Michigan's portion of media days wouldn't be limited to discussing Harbaugh and the potential he'd miss four games. Because the Big Ten stopped handling a vote for preseason conference rankings 13 years earlier, Cleveland.com took over and polled voters, mostly Big Ten beat writers, to produce an informal poll. Ohio State had been the Big Ten favorite each of the previous three years, but this time, Michigan, the two-time defending conference champion who had gone 25–3 the previous two seasons, was projected the Big Ten champion by a large margin. There were 37 voters, and 27 picked Michigan to win it all, while Ohio State received eight votes.

The Wolverines were a favorite in large part because of its defense but mostly because of McCarthy, the talented, athletic, returning starting quarterback. Harbaugh used his time during media days to build up his quarterback and referred to him as "once-in-a-generational" at Michigan. He described him as at the top of his game in every way and as a selfless teammate. Harbaugh said McCarthy was similar to Super Bowl–winning quarterback Patrick Mahomes and Josh Allen in the way they interact with their teammates and also in playmaking ability. Those were some pretty heady comparisons, but Harbaugh was supremely confident in McCarthy's ability and knew he was the quarterback he had always needed at Michigan since taking over in 2015.

"It's a tremendous honor to receive that praise from Coach Harbaugh, because I value his opinion so much," McCarthy said. "For me, personally, I take it as, 'Okay, that's great he thinks of me that way, but I eventually want to be better than those guys.' I want to be the best version of myself, whatever that is. I just focus on what abilities I have, what weaknesses I have, and how I can improve those weaknesses. I don't really get too much into comparisons because we're all unique, we're our own individuals. I'd like to think of myself as a player of that caliber one day, but right now I'm trying to focus on me."

Corum said he had seen McCarthy become incredibly focused and resistant to letting any talk of his talents flatter or fluster him. "J.J. is calm, cool, and collected," Corum said. "I don't think he lets stuff get to him. As any great player does, they don't let things fill up their head. J.J. is J.J., and J.J. will always be J.J. He's not gonna be a Patrick Mahomes, a Jalen Hurts, Josh Allen. He's not gonna be those guys. J.J.'s gonna be J.J. McCarthy, and I think he knows that. He doesn't want to be anyone else. I'm very excited to see where he goes this year. With a year under his belt, it's gonna get scary."

Harbaugh also had generated buzz about running a more balanced offense under Moore, his new coordinator. It had been around 60-40 run-pass during the 2022 season when Michigan finished fifth nationally in rushing, and Harbaugh and Moore wanted to see the offense go to more of a 50-50 split. McCarthy liked that plan. "In anything in life, when you have that perfect balance, you're gonna be successful," he said. "Adding that to our offense is gonna be tremendous for us."

Harbaugh, despite the NCAA drama, could not help feeling good about his team as the days neared the start of preseason camp. He knew what the Wolverines were made of, and for a second straight season, the nonconference schedule was weak, so while there would be criticism of their early opponents, it would give the team a chance to rotate in plenty of players to get game experience. That approach also allows the starters opportunities to rest late in games, and all of it combined typically pays off later in the season when the competition stiffens.

On a perfect final day of July, Harbaugh hosted the Champions Circle Golf Classic at Orchard Lake Country Club, featuring many of his players, the University of Michigan president Santa Ono, athletics director Warde Manuel, his assistant coaches and head coaches from other Michigan sports, and donors. This was an event to generate interest in the Champions Circle, the cornerstone of Michigan's name, image, likeness efforts. The players each joined a foursome, with McCarthy clearly a fan favorite. Later the players mingled, eager to begin preparations for the season with the start of camp.

"I'm feeling absolutely amazing about the season," McCarthy said during a break from golf that day. "I feel like I'm in such a good rhythm right now, mentally, physically, spiritually. I couldn't ask to be in a better spot."

McCarthy had gained 10 pounds since the end of the 2022 season, and his goals were to improve his efficiency in the pass game. He also wanted to use his legs more, making him a bigger threat and to become what he described as "an unstoppable force." He also shared how much he was enjoying working with new quarterbacks coach Kirk Campbell, who was elevated to the role after Matt Weiss, the previous co–offensive coordinator/quarterbacks coach, was fired once the University of Michigan police department began an investigation into a suspected computer crime in which he was allegedly involved. Campbell understood McCarthy better, and together they meshed.

Of course, there was more to the offense. The offensive line was expected to carry on the tradition of the previous two lines, winners of the Joe Moore Award, given to the nation's top offensive line. McCarthy couldn't help but gush about all the pieces around him on offense, including Corum and Edwards, tight ends Colston Loveland and transfer addition AJ Barner, and receivers Cornelius Johnson and Roman Wilson.

"I've never been on a team as talented as the one I'm on right now," McCarthy said.

Not only talented, but very much together. The defensive players solidified themselves as what they liked to describe as a brotherhood the previous season when Harbaugh dubbed them the "no-star" defense. That wasn't a knock and wasn't meant to say there weren't standouts. They simply adhered to a belief that no one was focused on individual awards, and they preached being one of 11—sort of an all-for-one, one-for-all approach. And there was a selflessness that permeated the team. When Valiant Management launched the One

More Year Fund earlier in the year to raise money to entice key players to return for one more season with the Wolverines rather than pursue the NFL, Corum was among the main targets. Offensive linemen Zak Zinter and Trevor Keegan and receiver Cornelius Johnson also were considering their futures, as were defensive tackle Kris Jenkins and linebacker Michael Barrett. The fund that raised more than $135,000 isn't the only reason they all decided to come back, but it helped. Corum, however, opted not to accept his portion and returned it to the pot to be distributed to his teammates.

"For many reasons," Corum said after the golf had concluded that day. "For me, I make a good amount just from marketing, and I know sometimes it can be hard for others—offensive line, defensive line, the guys that are in the trenches—to make money. I think they should get the marketing deals they deserve. Companies don't necessarily see it that way. They like the people who are flashy, the ones who score the touchdowns. For me, I wanted all my teammates to come back, and the One More Year Fund was perfect. I promoted it as much as I could. The rest of the guys that came back, they got a little something from it. It was good."

At that moment, Donovan Edwards walked over and playfully interrupted the one-on-one interview. "Still Lightning and Lightning," he said, beaming as he referred to the nickname coined in 2022 to describe the two of them. During the 2021 season, Hassan Haskins and Corum were referred to as "Thunder and Lightning," but "Lightning and Lightning" fit this running back tandem.

"It's the same, right?" Edwards asked Corum of the nickname.

"It's the same," Corum said, smiling. "Nothing changed."

"We're both electric, so why does one have to be Thunder?" Edwards said. "Lightning and Lightning has got a good ring to it, but how are we not the best duo in the country? We have one person go for 1,400, could have had 2,000 [in 2022]. You have another person who is 90 yards short of 1,000 yards. I rest my case."

Corum had been working hard coming off knee surgery after he suffered an injury in the final home game of the 2022 season. On the cusp of preseason camp, he described himself as feeling stronger than ever, which was saying a lot considering he had been long revered by his teammates for his devotion to the weight room. "I'm gonna be better than ever," Corum said. "I've been working my tail off to get to where I need to be, and I'm feeling great, mentally, physically, and I'm very excited. I haven't been this excited in a long, long time, and I've been playing since I was five. I'm more excited than ever because having football taken away from me, it gives you a new sense, not [of] urgency, but just the way you view it. You know it can be taken away at any given time, so I'm more excited than ever."

Preseason camp began with plenty of energy and confidence despite the issue with the NCAA and the expectation that Harbaugh would be suspended four games. Defensive coordinator Jesse Minter was busy trying to determine what would be the best rotation in the secondary, while Moore was working to establish the starting five on the offensive line. It was business as usual for the most part, until August 12—nearly three weeks after it had been reported that the negotiated resolution was the agreed-upon path—when multiple reports indicated that the negotiated resolution was no longer happening. There would not be a four-game suspension, however, and that meant in all likelihood the case would progress to eventually have Michigan and Harbaugh before the Committee on Infractions (COI) sometime in 2024. Also, there remained the possibility Michigan could self-impose penalties, including a similar suspension as a way to potentially ensure leniency from the NCAA.

Things had grown so tense with the NCAA that the organization, which is typically mum on investigations, uncharacteristically issued a statement. It attacked, in part, what had been messageboard chatter that this investigation was essentially "just about a cheeseburger"—the speculation being that Harbaugh had merely bought a cheeseburger for a recruit during the COVID dead period, so what's the big deal?

"The Michigan infractions case is related to impermissible on- and off-campus recruiting during the COVID-19 dead period and impermissible coaching activities—not a cheeseburger," Derrick Crawford, NCAA vice president of hearing operations, said in the statement. "It is not uncommon for the COI to seek clarification on key facts prior to accepting. The COI may also reject an NR [negotiated resolution] if it determines that the agreement is not in the best interests of the Association or the penalties are not reasonable. If the involved parties cannot resolve a case through the negotiated resolution process, it may proceed to a hearing, but the committee believes cooperation is the best avenue to quickly resolve issues."

Harbaugh's lawyer, Tom Mars, who had challenged the NCAA multiple times on transfer waivers and had never hidden his disdain for the organization, shot back. "Pursuant to the NCAA's internal operating procedures, and under threat of penalties, Michigan, the involved coaches, and their lawyers are prohibited from uttering a word about this ongoing case," he wrote in a Twitter (now X) post. "Yet the NCAA can issue a public statement putting its spin on the case?"

Nine days later on a Monday morning and less than two weeks from the start of the season, Harbaugh met with Warde Manuel. A team meeting was called for noon, and Harbaugh informed the players that he would serve a three-game, school-imposed suspension. It was a quick meeting with not much said. Harbaugh, who would be allowed to coach the team during the week, would miss the season opener September 2 against East Carolina, then games against UNLV and Bowling Green before returning to the sideline for the Big Ten opener against Rutgers.

"While the ongoing NCAA matter continues through the NCAA process, today's announcement is our way of addressing mistakes that our department has agreed to in an attempt to further that process," Manuel said in a statement. "We will continue to support Coach Harbaugh, his staff, and our outstanding student-athletes. Per the NCAA's guidelines, we cannot comment further until the matter is resolved."

This has been a strategy other programs have used. By getting out ahead of it and having a school-imposed suspension, it is generally considered a good-will effort in the hopes the NCAA won't add further penalties.

"I will continue to do what I always do and what I always tell our players and my kids at home, 'Don't get bitter, get better,'" Harbaugh said in a statement.

Defensive tackle Kenneth Grant said he was a bit surprised by Harbaugh's announcement about the suspension but suggested it would be a hiccup, at best, for the team. "It really doesn't affect us," he said. "The group of guys we've got, we're really resilient, so we're gonna come with even more firepower."

While Grant wouldn't share what Harbaugh said to the team after he informed the players of his suspension, it was clear this would serve as a source of motivation for the Wolverines. Grant said he expected the players to bring "some fire" to the field those first three games of the season as a way to show how much they rallied behind and valued their coach. The players reiterated Harbaugh's statement and insisted they would be better, not bitter.

There was no immediate indication of who would replace Harbaugh on the sideline those first three games. Would it be an interim head coach? Maybe a different coach each game? Curiously, in June at the high school football camp, Harbaugh made what he described as a bold statement that every one of his assistant coaches would become a head coach at some point. "I'd even say four after this season," he said. "The talent, the coaching acumen and talent is really good."

As the start of the season neared, players were still hanging onto the 51–45 loss to TCU in the College Football Playoff semifinal. The memory of the game had faded for the most part, but the disappointment lingered. As everyone knew, it was what pushed Michigan players during winter conditioning, spring practice, even preseason camp, and now as they closed in on the start of the season. Their goals were clear—beat Michigan State, Penn State, and Ohio State, win another Big Ten title, and then a national championship. Of course, that was enough to motivate them. But the heartbreaking loss to TCU had stung for months. It humbled them, but mostly it served as a constant reminder of the extra work and effort needed to avoid stumbling on their way to fulfilling their ultimate goal, a national championship.

"Something comes up in meetings where we watch a play we played against TCU, and you're like, 'Aw, shit,'" offensive lineman Karsen Barnhart said. "That's awful. It brings up bad memories, and then right after that you're just like, can't wait for Week 1, and you're excited."

No one dwelled on the loss because that would have been counterproductive, but they fed off it. It made them more focused and stronger mentally, and that was something they knew they'd have to rely on with their coach suspended. The players seemed unfazed by the off-field distractions, and Harbaugh mentioned several times that they were able to avoid getting caught up in any drama involving him because of their inner strength. It had to come from them, Harbaugh said, because it would be impossible to manufacture.

The Wolverines were ranked No. 2 in the Associated Press preseason poll. All they cared about was being ranked No. 1 in the final polls. That would always be the carrot dangling there at the end of a long season, but in the here and now, the players were all about being present. Be where your feet are, Corum and Sainristil preached to their teammates. Be in the moment. Don't look ahead. Don't look to the past. Be present.

"Don't think too far ahead," Corum said. "It's easy to think, 'Oh, yeah, we want to win a national title.' That's the bigger picture. We know what the bigger goals are. We just have to go day by day and enjoy it because we won't get this back. Embrace everything, enjoy it, be consistent, and be where our feet are."

On paper, there was a lot to like about this team, with so much talent returning on offense and defense. There was McCarthy and the running back duo, "Lightning and Lightning," plus a sophomore tight end in Colston Loveland, who the outgoing tight ends from the 2022 season said could very well be the best at the position in Michigan history. There was also an offensive line that added a few new pieces from the transfer portal but was following two straight Joe Moore Award–winning lines. Modern-era Michigan was noted for its dominant offensive lines. In the seven years before Harbaugh's arrival, that had not been the case but was something Harbaugh knew was vital to building the kind of physical offense he wanted. He wanted to talk about a balanced offensive attack, but the real balance was offense to defense and how they complemented each other. Michigan's defense was in its second season under Minter and third in the system Mike Macdonald had brought from the Ravens in 2021. There were strong players at each level of the defense with Jenkins in the interior of the defensive line, Braiden McGregor and Jaylen Harrell on the edges, Junior Colson and Michael Barrett at linebacker, and Will Johnson and Rod Moore in the secondary.

There was balance in the personnel but also balance among the teammates. This was a unified team from top to bottom, in every way.

"Whatever it is, if you are one strong unit, that is the most powerful force that is out there," McCarthy said. "That unity is the key fundamental reason for success. I feel like it's in the best spot it's ever been since I've been here, at least. It's gonna be threatened and there's going to be distractions and media trying to pull us to think we're something when we really haven't done anything. It's just making sure we stay focused with our tunnel vision day in, day out, consistent daily actions leading to our ultimate success. It's gonna come. Coach Herb [strength coach Ben Herbert] always harps on, we don't know when it's gonna come, but we're gonna be ready."

By adhering to the "be where your feet are" mantra, the Wolverines believed they could be ready for whatever adversity Herbert told them would undoubtedly be coming, whether on or off the field. But the veterans believed the culture that had been established in 2021 was intact and stronger than ever.

"That's the culture we've really ignited on the team and on the defense, and we stand by that," Jenkins said. "I mean, obviously, we got monsters, and we got guys on his team that are gonna dominate—you're gonna see them ball out and play on Sundays—but it's just we've identified that this is our team, we play together, we play for each other, we don't just play for ourselves. That's how we treat and we're gonna attack every single game. And the biggest mindset is, obviously, wearing a Block M, because you're gonna have everybody coming for, you're gonna have everybody trying to hunt you down. But we've just really tried to change that mentality.... We're going to start doing the hunting. And that starts with the first game of the season, that starts with getting to 15–0, and getting to areas where we haven't gotten there before. That starts now."

This was a group that felt so proven on the field that the intangibles were what they wanted to talk about. It had been established how close they all were. They did things together off the field, and there were no conflicts, no pettiness. A team can't win together without being together, and that's what they stressed. They applauded each other, praised each other. Some players had even picked up meditating regularly after observing McCarthy and the benefits he gained from it.

"If you live in the present moment, what we did in the past is not going to help us now," McCarthy said. "It's what we're doing right now. It's hard because it's so easy to fall back on that and just have this sense of confidence about ourselves that we did this, so obviously we'll be able to do this and more. No, it doesn't work like that. It could happen on any given Saturday where a team sneaks up on us and beats us on a last play. We're avoiding that from happening by continuing to do the things we do."

The players knew Harbaugh wouldn't be on the sideline for the first three games, and a little more than a week before the season opener, he announced that the head-coaching duties would be divided among four assistants. They would be the four names he hinted back in June would be head coaches sooner than later. Minter would coach Game 1. Game 2 against UNLV would be split between special-teams coordinator/safeties coach Jay Harbaugh, who would coach first half; and running backs coach/run game coordinator Mike Hart would lead the second half. Sherrone Moore would coach the prime-time game against Bowling Green. Harbaugh also announced that Herbert, the director of the strength staff, had a new title: associate head coach.

Moore would miss the first game of the season because of a one-game suspension, a penalty approved by the NCAA Committee on Infractions as part of a negotiated resolution relating to the NCAA investigation that included the impermissible visits during the COVID recruiting dead period. Newsome, whose name had surfaced in the investigation, would not face suspension.

With a plan in place, Harbaugh felt confident in the four coaches he entrusted with the game-day head-coaching duties.

"Because I know how good they are," Harbaugh said. "All 10 coaches, I believe, are tremendous and talented. I know each time that a coach is the head coach, I know the preparation is going to be the fullest, at the max. That's going to be the best thing for our football team. When you're the head coach during a game and you're the guardian of victory, that's a tremendous responsibility. You understand complementary football. It's not just defense. It's not just offense. It's not just about special teams, it's the whole team, and they're gonna be great at it."

Not one of the four fill-ins Harbaugh selected had college head-coaching experience. Harbaugh wasn't concerned. "I just watch how they approach it exactly how you would think they would," he said on the *Inside Michigan Football* radio show. "They are getting so prepared. This is the biggest game kind of [mentality], and it's been really good for our team. I just know what it is going to be like when it is their week and their day. They are going to coach great. They are going to coach their tails off."

Based on various assessments of Michigan's nonconference schedule, a fan could have been plucked out of Michigan Stadium to coach the first three games. Chris Low of ESPN said this was the easiest schedule among Power Five programs. Jerry Palm of CBS Sports called Michigan's schedule the cushiest in the Big Ten considering it was the only conference team without a Power Five nonconference opponent. Pat Forde of *Sports Illustrated* wrote that Michigan had the easiest September. "All things considered," Forde wrote, "a fine month to be suspended."

All of that schedule criticism had no effect on the players. After all, they weren't the ones scheduling the games. They just played them. "It don't matter who we're playing," McCarthy said. "It could be out in the parking lot right there. It could be at Yost [the ice hockey arena]. We're going to bring our all. Day by day, game by game, it doesn't matter who we're playing, we're going to give it our all."

– 3 –

THE SEASON OPENS

FINALLY, after all the buildup and the "Will he or won't he be suspended?" saga, it was game week of Michigan's season opener against East Carolina. Despite Harbaugh's suspension for the first three games, he would still prepare the team during the week, and he would still address media at a weekly Monday news conference that always began around noon in Schembechler Hall. Minter would also take questions as the acting head coach, but Harbaugh was the story, as he always was, and he didn't waste the opportunity to distract from the obvious questions about not being on the sideline. Instead, he presented a topic that ultimately gained legs nationally.

Harbaugh opened that news conference not talking about missing out on coaching the season opener or about East Carolina or his team and instead focused on what he described as the "big picture" of college football. He read from prepared notes and proceeded to speak more than six minutes before taking questions. Harbaugh, long an advocate for college athletes, shared his thoughts on the need for revenue-sharing in light of the enormous television deals and profits being made while the athletes playing the games aren't seeing a penny.

"[This is] much bigger than any one game, bigger than any game this season," Harbaugh said.

This wasn't the first time Harbaugh had advocated for college student-athletes and also wasn't his first foray into discussing the need for revenue-sharing with the athletes as expanding conferences receive bloated amounts of money from massive television deals. He brought up the idea of revenue-sharing in 2020 and again in 2022 at Big Ten media days, and said he wanted to use his platform to be a voice for athletes to encourage change.

"We have to try to make it work, we have to try to make it better and right now," Harbaugh said. "The current status quo is unacceptable and won't survive. In my opinion, we capitalize on the talent, we should pay the talent for their contributions to the bottom line."

Harbaugh had seen comments from then Notre Dame athletics director Jack Swarbrick, who appeared five days earlier on *The Dan Patrick Show* and described college football in its current state as a "complete disaster." Swarbrick suggested the decision-makers had lost their way in terms of focusing on student-athletes and what's best for them. Harbaugh could not have agreed more.

"What I don't understand is how the NCAA television networks, conferences, universities, and coaches can continue to pull in millions and, in some cases, billions of dollars in revenue off the efforts of college student-athletes across the country without providing enough opportunity to share in the ever-increasing revenues," he said passionately. "When student-athletes call it a game, the corporate types call it a business. When the student-athletes call it a business, corporate types call it a game."

Harbaugh said the current status quo would topple the sport. He spoke of the evolution of the game beginning in the 1970s when there were few games televised each week to now, with most games on network or cable television or a streaming service.

"In the major conferences, every game is nationally televised to millions of households and sold-out stadiums every Saturday," Harbaugh said. "Why wouldn't we let the student-athletes share in the success of their sport?... We all should be about diversity, equity, and inclusion. I'm calling for a system that is fair, equitable, and benefits all involved. Don't exclude the student-athletes from the profits. My opinion, you can't say you're about diversity, equity, and inclusion, if you aren't willing to include the student-athletes in revenue-sharing."

Harbaugh admittedly didn't have the answers or solutions to this but suggested the heavy hitters in college football, including the NCAA and TV network heads and conference commissioners, need to have conversations about the state of the sport and rewarding college athletes. He would revisit this topic much later in the season, but even though he didn't have the blueprint for a path forward and how to achieve what would be equitable for the players at the start of the season or later, he pledged to continue advocating for college athletes and revenue-sharing.

"It's got to change, and it's got to happen timely," Harbaugh said, firmly. "Now."

There was a general feeling by many college football fans and observers that Harbaugh took such a vocal stand on a controversial subject like revenue-sharing the week of the first game of his suspension as a way to attack and belittle the NCAA. But revenue-sharing is not just an NCAA issue and operates on so many different levels. Harbaugh had never shied away from questioning the NCAA and pushing for things like one-time transfers and finding rulebook loopholes—who can forget the satellite camps from early in his time at Michigan?—but this was not a petty swipe. It was, however, strategic. Harbaugh knew there would be plenty of eyes on this news conference and interest in what he said, the assumption that reporters would focus on the suspension, not to mention that Michigan was the preseason No. 2–ranked team. So Harbaugh used the opportunity to pound his fist for college athletes in the hopes of initiating constructive conversation, while also shining the light on him as the loudest advocate for change to benefit those playing the games.

While Harbaugh's feelings on revenue-sharing were definite, they were less so regarding the upcoming Saturday and how he might process not being on the sideline for the season opener. He wasn't going to make any predictions about how he might react, but this was not a small thing. Harbaugh, over the years, had shared several versions of how he envisioned his life unfolding—he was going to play football, then coach, then die, he'd say, with no deviation from that plan. Football had been his life for so long, not being on the field hadn't occurred to him. As a quarterback at Michigan, he had broken his arm and missed seven games, although he was able to return to the sideline. In the NFL, he rarely missed games due to injury. Harbaugh recalled having an MCL injury, wearing a brace and playing. He had a shoulder separation and missed two games.

"I've heard people comment it's a slap on the wrist," Harbaugh said of the three-game, school-imposed suspension. "It's more like a baseball bat to the kneecaps or to the shoulder. I equate everything to football. I've never missed three games unless it was for a broken arm or a dislocated shoulder."

He was also dealing with misinterpretations of the suspension. He said his wife, Sarah, had received calls from friends asking what they were going to do with the three-week vacation. "There isn't one," he said. "I'm coaching every single day."

Except on game days when he would not be permitted on the sideline or the stadium premises.

"It's definitely an unusual circumstance and unfortunate," running back Kalel Mullings said. "For us, the biggest thing is, in order to reach all the goals we want to reach, we have to win every single game every single week. And in order to do that we have to take each game week by week, play by play, game by game. The biggest thing to do that and reach our goals is just trying to make this unusual situation feel as normal as possible and try to not let the outside noise affect what we're doing here inside this building. At the end of the day, we're here for each other. We want to win and complete our goals for each other so all the stuff that's happening outside the building, things from people outside the building that are affecting people inside the building, we want to leave that to the side and focus on winning games. Just treating it as normal as possible, honestly."

Normal? Not exactly, but Harbaugh felt comfortable with his plan for the coaches each game, beginning with Minter handling the opener and quarterbacks coach Kirk Campbell filling in for Moore as the play caller. Harbaugh coined a new phrase—"guardians of victory"—to apply to the four coaches who would be acting head coaches. When you're a head coach during a game, Harbaugh said that in his mind you become the "guardian of victory," a tremendous responsibility because the head coach oversees the entire team and not just one facet. This would be an audition of sorts for the four assistant coaches and would give them a taste of the multiple game-day head-coaching duties.

Minter was eager for the opportunity. He had learned from his father, Rick Minter, a former head coach of the University of Cincinnati (1994–2003) and continued to lean on him since his father also was a defensive analyst at Michigan. As motivated as the players were after the loss to TCU, Minter felt just as responsible for the loss and, after reflecting on how the season ended, threw himself at taking the Michigan defense to a new level. More than ever, he wanted them focused on the four pillars that the players would reference throughout the season—block destruction, ball disruption, shocking effort, and obnoxious communication. Defensive tackle Mason Graham believed that completely embracing the four pillars was the biggest step the defensive players took in the off-season. Minter was about to be head coach for a game, but he was a defensive coordinator through and through.

It started with communication—the obnoxious kind—which would translate to the players being, as they often said, one of 11 with all of them working in sync. "Shocking effort" had to do with taking the best angles and precision tackling; "block destruction" was about shedding blockers, staying in plays, and ball disruption—that was a major focus of the off-season. Minter wanted more forced fumbles, pass breakups, and interceptions, preferably pick-sixes. Minter also made the four-pillars instruction about all the assistant coaches. Each had a pillar specialty. For instance, Mike Elston, the defensive line coach, worked with his linemen on block destruction, but he also taught it to the back-end players, the linebackers and defensive backs. Safeties coach Jay Harbaugh's pillar was ball disruption; linebackers coach Chris Partridge had shocking effort; and defensive backs coach Steve Clinkscale was in charge of obnoxious communication. Each taught the entire defense.

"We actually take a few moments between each meeting, each coach, and we present a little bit from our pillar in practice and in the game," Clinkscale said. "We do a quick-pillar four plays, we may do a long pillar, might be 15 or 20 plays. We also, in camp, we get a big slot of time to go over from every different way that you can pursue an angle or block destruction from each level. And we all watch it as an entire defense, so the D line know how we teach the DBs, the DBs know how we teach the D line, and they're all hearing it from one voice. Coach Minter, he gets all the credit for that, making that an importance. Anything in life where you stress it and make it important, that's what you end up doing well."

Minter and his staff also wanted more physicality on defense, more attack. Clinkscale described it as a bit more "recklessness" with the players' bodies going up and getting the ball and tackling more physically and finishing plays more decisively.

This week would not give Minter a full look at how it is to be a head coach, considering Harbaugh would be there at practices and game planning and doing the day-to-day. He knew he wouldn't have to keep his finger on the pulse of everything it takes to prepare for a game, but Minter was preparing himself for his game-day role by making certain Campbell and Jay Harbaugh, the special teams coordinator, knew he trusted their decisions in those phases. As far as Minter's game-day decision-making, he made no predictions but referenced Harbaugh's comment about being a "guardian of victory" and said that was the responsibility he felt. He planned to coach within his leadership style, make sure the Wolverines played at a high level with his stamp on the team.

"I'm really excited because I know the capabilities of the coaching staff we have," Minter said. "Coach has said it, just about the all the coaches having the capabilities of being in this position one day. He's an advocate for us. This is him advocating for his staff and putting us all in a position to get this experience first and foremost, [to] know what it's like to be a head coach. Just makes you want to go prove him right while he's willing to do that for multiple people on staff. I think it's a really cool and unique thing."

With Harbaugh still able to do his job during the week, the players didn't detect a disruption in their football schedules. "It's felt like normal practice," center Drake Nugent said. "It's like nothing happened."

The season opener was wildly anticipated, not because of Michigan's opponent, East Carolina, but because it was the start of what fans believed could be a special season. This was for Harbaugh, in his ninth season coaching his alma mater, his best team and his best chance at a national championship. Even the oddsmakers seemed to be believers in the Wolverines. According to Bet MGM, they had the fourth-best odds to win the national championship.

When the Michigan team buses arrive outside Michigan Stadium in front of the locker room, there are always rows of fans on the stairs along where the players and coaches walk. They cheered them on as Minter, not Harbaugh, was among the first off the bus with Kris Jenkins just to his left. Corum and Zinter appeared, wearing T-shirts with HARBAUGH in large letters across the top and a number of images of their coach from his quarterback playing days featured. It was McCarthy, though, who took the tribute to his head coach to a new fashion level. He walked off the bus wearing a navy T-shirt in reverse so that the HARBAUGH stripped across what would be the shoulders, was now on his upper chest with Harbaugh's jersey No. 4 below. McCarthy then used what looked like a piece of wide white athletic trainer's tape and wrote FREE in blue and placed it above Harbaugh's name.

It didn't end with doctored T-shirts. In the second series of the game, the Michigan players lined up in the train formation, McCarthy walked alongside them, and each raised four fingers above their heads to honor their coach before settling into their normal set. "That was definitely a tribute to Coach Harbaugh," McCarthy said. "That was pretty cool to do that."

Michigan won with ease, defeating East Carolina 30–3, losing out on the shutout at the end of the game as ECU made a 33-yard field goal. McCarthy missed only four of his 30 attempts and had 280 yards with three touchdowns, all to Roman Wilson. The bonus was McCarthy sat the fourth quarter, allowing Davis Warren to take over. Corum had 73 rushing yards on 10 carries and a touchdown, and James Turner, who grew up in nearby Saline and transferred from Louisville before the season, added a 50-yard field goal. Turner missed an extra point and a 52-yard field-goal attempt.

After the game, it was clear Harbaugh was on the players' minds.

"I wasn't expecting it to be that much different, but personally [it] just felt like something was missing today, and it was definitely him," McCarthy said. "He has this presence that it's all about winning, all about competing, all about pushing through. Just as simple as the pregame speech, I was missing that voice."

"Yeah, me, too," Corum, sitting to McCarthy's left at the post-game table, chimed in.

McCarthy added, "It really sucked going out there the first game, him not being out there because he put as much blood, sweat, and tears into this, as much as we have. So it's unfortunate, but we know we get him back Week 4, and he's gonna be hungrier than ever."

Corum texted Harbaugh before the game. "I said, 'Play as hard as you can, as fast as you can, and don't worry,'" Corum said. "That's what he tells us before the game. Like J.J. said, I miss hearing that. It kind of gets me pumped up. After that I said, 'We got you, Coach,' and he said, 'I know you do.' It was definitely different, but Coach Minter did a great job stepping in as the head coach today, but I can't wait to get Coach Harbaugh back."

Minter said it hit him Friday night after talking to Harbaugh for the last time before the game that he would be the head coach for Game 1. "Like this is going down," Minter said. "And I was excited for the opportunity, and I was just really excited to see our guys play. Proud of the way they played. I thought Coach Campbell did a great job calling the plays. To [ECU's] credit, they were putting 11 guys up there and trying to stop the run. I thought as the game went on, we did a really good job just sort of taking what was there, taking what they gave us. I think for the most part through three quarters, we really played the game on our terms, on our tempo. We controlled the ball at times with the passing game, at times with the running game."

The two coaches who weren't on the sideline, Harbaugh and Moore, watched the game on Peacock, a streaming service that Harbaugh couldn't quite figure out how to access, at Moore's home. They had Panera sandwiches courtesy of Moore's wife, Kelli, and kept close tabs on how the team played and the coaches coached.

"As Sherrone and I were sitting there, it was kind of like, 'Time for a play-action pass. Let's run this,'" Harbaugh said. "It was uncanny how many times that's what Kirk would call or do. We both said to each other, 'Time to get the starters out,' and the starters were out. It was cool that way."

Harbaugh also appreciated the tributes from the players. "I just felt the love from them just doing them," he said. "I could see it in our players. I could see it in our coaches. And that's what I want them to do, I want them to do them. 'Be you,' is the way we say it around here. I saw them having fun."

The team persevered without him, but it was clear this wasn't something they wanted to get used to. Harbaugh kept up positive appearances for the players, but as he said, he equates everything to football, and not being able to coach the next two Saturdays would be a challenge.

– 4 –

GUARDIANS OF VICTORY

HARBAUGH digested how he felt the first Saturday of his three-game suspension and said it was about turning "the negative into the positive." He said he put the needs of the players and coaches ahead of his own while doing the absolute best he could. His routine didn't change on game day. He got up early, did the things he normally did, except, of course, his lifeline, coaching.

What he missed was the competition.

"You really feel that," Harbaugh said on his weekly Monday night radio show. "It's like anybody on the team, player, coach, myself. You put your blood, sweat, and tears into that preparation, into those practices, into the team on a daily, weekly basis. Because of that, you feel like you are there. Same thing I know as a dad, I know as a coach, the needs of the team are what's most important. Your needs are very secondary. It's tough not to be there, tough not being part of the competition, but you know they're getting to do it. It makes me happy."

Harbaugh would have to spend the next two Saturdays being tested in this way that was so against his grain, but he was giving an opportunity to his assistants. For the upcoming UNLV game, his son,

Jay Harbaugh, was going to coach the first half, and Hart, the running backs coach, would get the second. Jay Harbaugh likened not having his father on the sideline to missing a family member during a family gathering. You find a way to carry on, he said, and the return simply becomes more anticipated.

It was an odd setup with two head coaches handling the game, but Harbaugh and Hart said they would take a collaborative approach. Their offices were next to each other, they respected each other, and earlier in the year during the spring game, they already had fun together on opposite sides as Hart's team defeated Harbaugh's. They were determined during the week to work together, and the plan would be to consult each other throughout the game to decide on aggressiveness in different situations, such as a fourth-down call.

Both men have aspirations of being head coaches, and both had coordinator titles, Harbaugh with special teams and Hart as run-game coordinator. Harbaugh had become well known as the Swiss Army knife of the staff, having coached tight ends, running backs, and safeties, while always working with special teams. Hart, who had been a running backs coach at his previous stop, Indiana, also was associate head coach there and had a taste of the administrative aspects of being a head coach. What seemed like a typical path to being a head coach was being an offensive or defensive coordinator. Hart has never been of that opinion, had never put himself on a trajectory to being an offensive coordinator, and believed the move could be made from position coach to head coach.

"I think the path is different," Hart said the week of the game. "If you look at coaches now, it's a lot different. I think anybody can be a head coach no matter what you do. It comes down to leadership and management. You have to deal with different things [as head coach], you have to do different things. I think that as long as you can lead people and you're organized, you can be a head coach. That's what it comes down to. Motivation, leadership, and belief. People have to believe in you. When you have those things and you have those characteristics, anybody can be a head coach."

For the players, it seemed like it was back to the normal in the sense the conversation wasn't so much about not having Harbaugh on the sideline but about actual football. For months they had talked about spring practice, then preseason camp, then game-week practices heading into the opener and Harbaugh's suspension, and finally they had a game to dissect and discuss. And frankly, coming out of the season opener without a sack was pretty much the only complaint among the players. They vowed to change that against UNLV.

"We definitely weren't satisfied with what we did as an edge rush unit," Braiden McGregor said. "We think that we have the best room in the country. Going out there and not being able to put any sacks on the board was frustrating, but we're gonna get back in the film room and take it day by day and keep getting better. We're so hungry, we all want sacks, we all want stats, we all want to eat."

Game day was as much about Harbaugh not being there as it was about the team playing its second game, and everyone wanted to know where he'd be watching and what he'd be doing. A week earlier, he and wife, Sarah, were responsible for bringing Gatorade and snacks to their son Jack's youth football game. But this Saturday morning, Harbaugh worked the chains for the game, and the Ann Arbor Saints earned a much-needed victory. They went home, and Harbaugh cut the front lawn before the game. He watched his team play on television along with his daughter Katie and son Johnny, and at halftime went to McDonald's. After the game, he cut the backyard grass. This was the new (temporary) normal.

Jay Harbaugh led the team to a 21–0 lead at halftime, and then Hart took over as they combined to lead the team to a 35–7 victory, again allowing a late score. McCarthy kept up his precision passing and completed his first 13 passes, finishing 22-of-25 for 278 yards and two touchdowns. It was a bittersweet day for him as he honored his childhood friend, Ryan Keeler, who was on the UNLV team but died in February from a fatal arrhythmia. McCarthy wrote Keeler's jersey No. 47 on his left hand to honor him during the game and did not know until after the game that his second touchdown throw to Wilson was a 47-yarder. Corum ran for three touchdowns, and Wilson caught both of the touchdown receptions. The defense turned things up and recorded five sacks, Jaylen Harrell and Kenneth Grant each credited with one sack and one assist.

"We were a little frustrated knowing we didn't have any sacks or too many pressures," Harrell said, referring to the season opener. "So all week we honed in, like, 'We've got to get back there today,' so we just trusted the game plan."

Michigan had decided that the win or loss in the first three games would be credited to the coaches, so Harbaugh and Hart each got a win. "Pretty easy for us to be able to step in just because it's a well-oiled machine," Jay Harbaugh said. "It's running really well."

With the win, Hart would become the first Black head coach at Michigan to win a game. It was incredibly meaningful for Hart, Michigan's all-time leading rusher. "It's a great honor," Hart said. "I had a chance to play for Tony Dungy, had a chance to play for Jim Caldwell. My first coaching job was with Ron English at Eastern Michigan. We have an athletics director in Warde Manuel who's African American, I've had a close relationship since he's been here. So I just had a lot of great coaches who are African American that I've had the chance to look up to, and just really let me know that it can happen, that it's a possibility. Hopefully we see more African American coaches in college football. We need more. So hopefully I'll be one of those one day."

Hart then quickly corrected himself.

"I *will* be one of those one day," he said.

There was a lot for Harbaugh to praise on Monday as the Wolverines began preparations for Bowling Green, coached by former Michigan quarterback and quarterbacks coach Scot Loeffler.

McCarthy, through six quarters (since he'd sat out the fourth quarters of the first two games), had completed 87.3 percent of his passes. He had missed on only seven of 55 attempts. There was some hand-wringing among fans, though, regarding the run game. Michigan had 301 rushing yards through two games and four touchdowns. Harbaugh reminded everyone that a year earlier, the concern was the pass game was lagging behind the run game. "This year, the passing game is hitting on all cylinders," he said. "The goal is for J.J. to be the best quarterback in the country on the best football team. We gotta get that in the run game, too. I want the best backs on the best team as well. I know we're gonna get there. Excited to make that happen, and it'll be a great emphasis on that because we're capable."

It was time for Moore to take over as acting head coach for the Wolverines in the night game against the Falcons, who were more than five-touchdown underdogs. But the final tune-up before the start of the Big Ten schedule wasn't on par with the previous two games, and after the buildup from Harbaugh about his quarterback, McCarthy proceeded to throw three interceptions in the Wolverines' 31–6 win.

"I'm going to take all those on the chin, put them all on me," McCarthy said after the game. "There's a lot of stuff that didn't go my way, didn't go the offense's way. I can't wait to watch the tape and see the mistakes that were made and get better from it, honestly."

Corum broke the 100-yard barrier for the first time in the season and had 101 yards and two touchdowns. McCarthy had touchdown passes to Wilson and a circus-catch touchdown by Cornelius Johnson. On a flea-flicker in the third quarter, McCarthy threw deep down field to Johnson, who was covered by Bowling Green defensive back Davon Ferguson. The play had been installed earlier that week, but certainly wasn't planned to play out the way it did. McCarthy's throw was tipped three times, including off Ferguson's helmet after Johnson's first tip, before Johnson secured the catch by his right hip.

"Got a couple of lucky bounces, but I was able to just stay focused there and work on that concentration," Johnson said. "It wasn't what I was expecting, but those reps of focusing on the JUGS machine, getting those extra catches after practice, it all pays off."

Michigan had four turnovers, including one on special teams, but the defense dominated again and caused two turnovers that led to points. Jenkins and Quinten Johnson each had an interception.

"Guys being the difference maker, guys stepping up," Harbaugh would say later of the defense. "Calling it 'guardians of victory' now. Kris Jenkins, the interception he made. The way Jaylen Harrell is playing. Again, another week where he's the tone-setter that caused a fumble, tackles, had the rush, had the pressure that led to an interception. Tremendous. Quinten Johnson, a guardian of victory, squashed the momentum right before the half there."

And for McCarthy, the takeaway was that he still had plenty on which to work. On his third interception against Bowling Green, he was actually trying to throw it away, but McCarthy didn't get enough velocity on the throw, and it was low enough to get picked off. He said he had done the same thing in practice, where he throws it "too close," taking too much of a chance. "This one's gonna be a perfect lesson to learn from," McCarthy said. "And it's never gonna happen again."

That's exactly what Harbaugh wanted to hear as the Wolverines headed into the start of the Big Ten season with his highly anticipated return to the sideline.

– 5 –

THE BIG TEN
SEASON KICKS OFF

THAT MICHIGAN was 3–0 after the conclusion of the nonconference schedule was hardly shocking, considering the Wolverines' opponents were so clearly overmatched. They outscored the teams a combined 96–16, even while the starters sat for most of the fourth quarters. That the Wolverines were able to stay so locked in despite the unconventional nature of their game days without Harbaugh was also maybe not so remarkable, considering the leadership from the upperclassmen. But his absence also seemed to give them an edge and that proverbial chip on their shoulder.

For Harbaugh, missing the three games was a gut punch. "I went to a place I've never been," he said, "which wasn't on the sideline."

He did learn a few things during his three-game absence to apply to his coaching. Watching on television offered a new perspective, different from the game film they break down and study and gave him new eyes on what goes on during a game that he doesn't generally see while coaching. Also a product of his watching the first three games, Harbaugh wondered whether the players put too much pressure on themselves in terms of how many points they scored and margin of victory.

"You watch the game and so many feelings of, 'Hey, just win. Just win the game,'" Harbaugh said. "By one point, is what we're really after."

He also found himself, after hoping for no player injuries, feeling what he described as greedy. He wanted the Michigan defense to be the best, the offense to be the best, special teams to be the best. Then he narrowed his focus to position groups earning that label and then, of course, he wanted individual players to realize their greatness and have others notice that, as well.

"That's what we want to be about," Harbaugh said. "So we're gonna chase that and we're gonna keep chasing that perfection."

"Perfection" is not how McCarthy's performance against Bowling Green might have been described, certainly not with three interceptions and certainly not after missing only seven passes his first two games. But this is where there were signs of players speaking up and having the backs of their teammates. McCarthy was the first to admit he had an off, less-than-perfect game, but Corum stepped up to defend his quarterback as the Wolverines began preparations for Rutgers. There is such a thing, he said, as an "off" game, and that while everyone pursues perfection, that's rarely, if ever, achieved. But off games happen to everyone.

"Kobe [Bryant] had off games, LeBron [James] has off games, Tom Brady, he's had off games," Corum said when he was asked about the concept of an off game relating to what McCarthy had just gone through. "It's a game at the end of the day. It's a game. Sometimes you could say it's luck if you have a good game. Is it luck? Or is it just you're good at what you do? You have off games as a player. The defense prepared for you really well, you might have made a mistake that you usually don't make, stuff happens.

"It's just about how you go about it. Do you learn from it? Do you make the same mistake over and over again? Or do you fix it? I'll tell you something about this team, when we make a mistake, we tend to fix it right away. So, yeah, players have off games. I've had plenty of off games in my career since youth ball. It's just part of the game, and as long as you learn from it, is it really an off game? It may be to media, but you learn from it, you get better from it, and that's what I try to preach to my teammates, even to myself: just learn from your mistakes and be better."

Corum's response was an early indication of just how tight these players were. They got the win, they were unbeaten, and everyone had things to work on, not just McCarthy.

There had been plenty of criticism of Michigan's nonconference schedule, but they did what good teams are supposed to do. They dominated the opponents and allowed for younger and less-experienced players to get important game reps, always an important step in a long season. Rutgers coach Greg Schiano had taken notice of Michigan and knew that no matter the strength of the opponents the Wolverines had defeated, this team was legit.

"No. 2 team in the country. Probably could be easily ranked No. 1," Schiano told Rutgers reporters. "They're that good, and there's absolutely no weaknesses in this team."

Schiano knew how complete Michigan was, and he also knew how fired up the players would be with Harbaugh returning to the sideline. Corum had spoken about what it would feel like to head down the Lloyd Carr Tunnel at Michigan Stadium with his head coach for the first time this season, and the players brimmed with excitement.

The Scarlet Knights opened the scoring with a three-play, one-minute scoring drive, highlighted by a 69-yard touchdown pass. Mike Sainristil had slipped and believed he was the reason Rutgers was able to make the big play.

"That was my man that scored," Sainristil said. "Good players make good plays, good players make mistakes. He scored a touchdown. I kind of brushed it off right away. I said, 'I'm gonna get you all one back.'"

That would be all the scoring for Rutgers, and Michigan earned its fourth win of the season and first in Big Ten play, 31–7. McCarthy was 15-of-21 for 214 yards and a touchdown pass to freshman Semaj Morgan. Corum scored two rushing touchdowns, Turner added a field goal, and Sainristil did get one back with a pick-six in the third quarter. Sainristil said he told defensive backs coach Steve Clinkscale coming out of halftime that he was going to get an interception, and that's what he did, returning it 71 yards for the score.

Michigan's defensive backs were playing man and wanted to be aggressive. That's when Sainristil jumped the route and picked off Gavin Wimsatt. After making the catch, linebacker Junior Colson appeared to almost collide with Sainristil, but instead was flipped. "Flipped me in the air," Colson said, laughing. "I was so excited for that. He's earned it. He works his butt off every day. You see him practice, he gets picks in practice. It wasn't new to me. He's always been getting picks."

For Harbaugh, it was like being home. Corum said after the game that players relished hearing Harbaugh's pregame speech and that he simply "brings the juice." Harbaugh was giddy after the game.

"Everybody kept saying, 'Welcome back, welcome back,'" he said. "I never really left, but I wasn't where I was supposed to be. It was great to be back in there in the action where the competition is. That's always been the best part for me, playing football, and second best is being able to coach it. Nowhere I'd rather be than on the sideline coaching our team. I was happy. I really wanted that win. Our players, they wanted more. You could just tell by the way they were playing and how happy they were. Coach wanted it, but players wanted even more."

After four straight games at home, it was time for Michigan to hit the road for the first of back-to-back road games, starting with Nebraska. Road games no longer felt daunting to the Wolverines, not since the 2021 season when they decided to take over the opponents' stadiums. It started at Wisconsin that season during the Camp Randall "Jump Around" tradition between the third and fourth quarters. That's when the Wolverines memorably began jumping around on the sideline joining the fans in the stadium. A week later in an epic Memorial Stadium night-game environment in Lincoln, Nebraska, the Michigan players danced on the sideline to AC/DC's "Thunderstruck," the stadium bathed in a red lightshow. The Wolverines were trailing at the time but soaked in the vibe and played air guitar before going on to win the game. In 2022 at Iowa, the Michigan players dismissed the famous pink visitors' locker room and waved pink towels on the sideline. They did that, they did all of it to let the opposing teams and fans know they didn't care, and they weren't fazed.

"Road games are probably my favorite," McCarthy said the week of the Nebraska game. "I love the Big House, and it's an amazing atmosphere, but there's something about going into someone else's building and hearing all the boos and feeling all the hate. I'm getting chills right now. It just brings a different spark and ignites a different fire inside of us. And there's nothing better than going into a stadium that's jumping and going crazy, and then by halftime, it's as quiet as a mouse. That's what we're going to try to do this weekend."

McCarthy was also feeling confident, having regained his form against Rutgers after the three-interception performance against Bowling Green. Not only did he throw for 214 yards and a touchdown, he also ran for 51 yards on seven carries, an important wrinkle in Michigan's offense. McCarthy referred to the Bowling Green game as a blessing in disguise and that he used it to fuel him in practice heading into the Big Ten opener. "The biggest thing I learned from it is not to put so much pressure on myself," he said. "I've just put an unrealistic expectation for that game. When one thing went wrong, the pressure, I really felt it, and I've never felt that before."

It was unusual to hear McCarthy speak about feeling pressure, since he always exuded supreme confidence. But whatever it was he experienced in that that game, he believed it was already helping him and would help him handle the rest of the season. Heading into Nebraska against a defense that ranked No. 1 nationally against the run, it seemed that McCarthy would have to be relied on to throw the ball and keep the offense humming, so this was a good time for him to be feeling good about his ability.

That's not how the game at Nebraska unfolded, however. McCarthy was efficient and missed only four of his 16 attempts for 156 yards and two touchdowns, both to Roman Wilson, whose first score was a thing of beauty. During the Wolverines' first drive against the Cornhuskers, Wilson jumped high over safety Isaac Gifford to make the touchdown reception in an unconventional way as he used Gifford's helmet to secure the catch. McCarthy found Wilson in the end zone on the 29-yard throw, and Wilson came down with the ball against Gifford's helmet in the highlight-reel moment.

"When J.J. threw it, I thought it was gonna be perfectly right over their head, but I think the wind might have taken it a little bit," Wilson said. "It was right behind the guy so I could see clear as day. Went up and grabbed it and the dude's head was in between me and the ball. I'm not sure where he was going, so I just brought it down with me."

A few days later, Wilson would share that he didn't think that was his best catch of the season. "I had one practice in this off-season, and I caught it one-handed. It's crazy stuff," Wilson said. "I don't know, maybe one day I'll show the world, but Coach Harbaugh says we're not allowed to post practice film so you guys might not ever see it."

What Michigan fans got to see, aside from another defensive tackle, this time Kenneth Grant, grab an interception, was a run game that would gouge the nation's No. 1 run defense. The Wolverines gained 249 yards on 51 carries and had touchdown runs by McCarthy, Corum, and Mullings. That kind of production was just what the offensive linemen had set out to achieve. The coaches had challenged the linemen in practice, and the players were focused on attacking the Cornhuskers' strength.

"When we see they're the No. 1 rushing defense, and they had a good rushing attack themselves, when you're in meetings, you take it a lot more serious," left guard Trevor Keegan said. "There's a little extra oomph. They did have the No. 1 rushing defense, but everybody played pass against them [the first four games], and we kinda knew that. They play a multitude of fronts and pressures we haven't seen. It's a rare defense. The way we prepared for it took care of itself."

After the Wolverines' first road win and their record now at 5–0, Keegan became more serious about the team and the season. "We knew coming in the off-season, complacency was going to be our biggest threat," he said. "There's not many guys on this team that are complacent. We came back, a lot of guys came back, we could have [gone] to the NFL and pursued our dreams. We came back to get this thing rolling and we worked our tails off. The way we work, the way we train, the way we practice, the way we prepare, we're pretty damn confident about it."

Keegan spoke of Ben Herbert, the team's director of strength and conditioning, as a critical piece of the puzzle. Herbert was so valued that Harbaugh had elevated him before the season to associate head coach. A year earlier, Harbaugh had wanted to nominate Herbert for the Broyles Award, given to the nation's top assistant, but he couldn't because the nominee has to be a field coach. More than once he described Herbert as the team's "X factor."

Herbert, or "Coach Herb," as the players referred to him, had shaped the players physically but also mentally. Harbaugh hired Herbert in 2018 and was immediately in awe of his level of detail.

In Herbert, he had found someone who combined an old-school strength coach with a cutting-edge, scientific strength coach. Harbaugh had always found you'd get one or the other in a strength coach, but Herbert had it all. Keegan mentioned Herbert after the Nebraska win, but it would not end there because Herbert would be cited time and time again.

"I was here back in the dump days in COVID [in 2020], that's what I call it," Keegan said. "If you're not winning this game, it's not worth it. When you're winning, you come in the building, everyone is smiling. When you're losing, it's pretty terrible. There's not any smiles on anyone's faces. The complete change was just the mindset. Back in 2020, it was, 'We can, we can win this game, we can do it.' And now it's, 'We will do it.' Our mentality, Coach Herb engraving that in our heads, it's really paid dividends. I think we're rolling right now. Five games win streak, rolling."

The Wolverines were, indeed, rolling and at 2–0 in the Big Ten had to travel to Minnesota for a night game. Harbaugh has been known for his sometimes unusual explanations, for his use, and at times, misuse of metaphors. On the Monday of practice week to go play for the Little Brown Jug, he shared how he's aware that when things are going well for a team, it doesn't take much to disrupt them. He channeled Sir Isaac Newton to explain the law of gravity as it applies to a football team. "When things are scary good, that's where you want to be, that's who you want to be with, that's how you want to be doing things," he said. "But the law of averages says that it's gonna catch up to you and to see if we could defy Sir Isaac Newton's laws of gravity—what goes up, must come down. And the gravitational force of the Earth is tremendous. And so are some of the forces against a football team, some of the things that are set there to divide a football team. The ones that aren't divided are the ones that are playing in the playoffs and, eventually, champion."

What can disrupt a team, as Harbaugh indicated, are things like jealousy, the star system, the media, injuries, and selfishness. In other words, human nature.

"You just have to keep those balls up in the air," Harbaugh said. "How do you keep them high? High energy, energy and working at it and attacking it. It's the only way to keep a balloon up that doesn't have helium in it, right? Eventually, it's gonna come down. But, hey, smoke still rises. It stays up a long time, I've noticed. Heat energy, those things are the way we're going about it."

The Wolverines kept those balls in the air at Minnesota as they played to retain the Little Brown Jug, the oldest trophy in college football. The truth is, they caught plenty of them. Cornerback Will Johnson gave Michigan its first points with a 36-yard interception return, and as the defensive players scrambled on the sideline to take their "Turnover Buffs" photo—whoever caused a turnover donned a pair of Cartier sunglasses, called Buffs, and a photo would commemorate the moment—this time Harbaugh was pulled into the shot.

Michigan smothered Minnesota 52–10 as McCarthy accounted for three touchdowns, including tight end Colston Loveland's only target, a 24-yard touchdown catch. The defense had two interceptions returned for touchdowns by Johnson and Keon Sabb. Defensive tackle Mason Graham, who had missed the prior two games because of broken left hand, returned to the starting lineup wearing a club on the hand and led the team with six tackles, including a sack. Michigan did not have any turnovers and had only one penalty a week after remarkably going penalty-free.

Sainristil was the first to grab the Jug and held it above his head, celebrating. Jenkins got a hold of it and walked along the edge of the front row of Michigan fans to allow them to touch the Jug. Michigan had outgained Minnesota 432 to 169 to improve to 6–0 at the halfway point of the season, and the Wolverines played all but one of the 75 players who traveled to Minnesota.

"They're as good as advertised," Minnesota coach P.J. Fleck said. "I think they're the best football team I've seen in 11 years of being a head coach. I've never seen a football team like that, that deep. They're one of the deepest teams, one of the best teams, one of the biggest teams, fastest teams, strongest teams, and they do not make mistakes. They are truly like a boa constrictor, and they do not beat themselves. They're very good at each position. They're very aligned with everything that they do. They know who they are, and they go and execute that game plan. There were times they did it at will tonight."

The Wolverines had been squeezing the life out of teams, Fleck was right about that. Through their first three Big Ten games, they had outscored teams 128–24. But still, there was the constant chatter that they really hadn't played a tough team. Overall, they had rolled opponents 224–40 and were ranked No. 1 nationally in scoring defense, yielding an average of 6.7 points per game. Rutgers, Nebraska, and Minnesota were led by quarterbacks who ranked at the bottom of the conference statistics, but to Michigan's credit, it had won two straight on the road. Still, the competition wasn't getting any stiffer, considering the Wolverines were about to host Indiana.

"Whatever is being said, we're just trying to get good at football," Harbaugh said. "Don't really pay too much attention to what's being said, good or bad. It's just about us. Want to talk about any subject, sounds like complacency was one earlier, the only antidote for any kind of things, good or bad, is leadership, character, that unyielding commitment to the basics and fundamentals of Michigan football, and a faith in each other. We'll continue to keep attacking. Whether it's the preparation, the meetings, the training, the practice, the games, just do the best we can. That's all we can ask of ourselves and our teammates."

As is often the case when a team is steamrolling opponents, questions at news conferences can take on a whole new focus. There had been considerable speculation that contract negotiations had picked up between Michigan and Harbaugh, in his ninth season at Michigan. On Monday of Indiana week, talk turned to whether he would be open to a revised contract. Earlier in the year, when Harbaugh was in conversation with the Denver Broncos about their head-coaching job, and not long after Michigan received a draft of a notice of allegations from the NCAA, University of Michigan president Santa Ono posted on X that Harbaugh would be staying.

"I just got off the phone with Coach Harbaugh and Jim shared with me the great news that he is going to remain as the Head Coach of the Michigan Wolverines," Ono wrote on January 16. "That is fantastic news that I have communicated to our athletics director Warde Manuel. #GoBlue."

Then a message from Harbaugh was posted on the official Michigan football account.

"I love the relationships that I have at Michigan—coaches, staff, families, administration, President Santa Ono, and especially the players and their families," Harbaugh's statement read. "My heart is at the University of Michigan. I once heard a wise man say, 'Don't try to out-happy, happy.' Go Blue!"

Harbaugh did not, however, begin the season with a contract extension. Maybe this would finally be the time that happened. "Like anybody, I've said it, you want to be somewhere where you're wanted," Harbaugh said when asked about the potential for a revised contract. "If they like what you do and how you do it, your bosses tell you that and then that gets reflected in a contract. Bottom line, any of us, right, we want to be somewhere they like how you do it and what you do."

Harbaugh was asked if he feels wanted at Michigan. "Yeah, I do," he said.

There had been flirtations with the NFL in recent years. He went to Minneapolis for an interview with the Vikings on national signing day in 2022, and earlier in 2023 had serious conversations with the Broncos. After he returned from Minneapolis without a job offer, Harbaugh signed a five-year, $36.7 million contract good through 2026. But at the beginning of the 2023 season, his annual compensation ranked fourth in the Big Ten, with Ohio State's Ryan Day leading the way. Harbaugh was asked during Indiana week if he had any contract discussions or assurances from Michigan.

"That's been kind of a three-and-a-half-year thing, what that is," Harbaugh said. "Eventually gets put into a contract. I can't say that any more clearly, and [I'm] definitely open to that. I think I've shown that through the years. Like anybody, man, I'm concentrating on and focused on having a good practice today. Got a team meeting coming up. We've got practices. It's coach-the-team-time when you're in the middle of the season."

Michigan athletics director Warde Manuel responded to a text from the *Detroit News*, which requested his response to Harbaugh's desire for a new contract. "I hope to make that a reality in the very near future," he said.

With Harbaugh's contract discussions apparently moving in a direction he found favorable, the focus returned to the Wolverines and their upcoming game against Indiana. What had become a positive for Michigan was the fact the comfortable leads allowed for the starters to rest late in the games. And that, in turn, made for more spirited practices. Michigan practiced hard on Tuesday, Wednesday, and Thursday, with rest on Friday before the game.

"We've done a good job on Saturdays [when], as a team, we go and we do what needs to be done," Sainristil said. "We handle business the way it should, which allows the starters, the [first and second strings] to be able to go into Tuesday and Wednesday practices with fresh bodies. So now you could go out there and you can give your all that practice. You can practice harder because I feel like the harder practices are, the easier games are, and I feel like that's something that we've done very well here for these first seven games."

Corum could not stress enough how much fresher his body felt because he could sit out the fourth quarters of games. Michael Barrett said he felt like he was able to focus on consistency during the week. Because they arrived Tuesday more rested coming off a game, he said they were able to get what he called "game moments" in practices.

After winning in back-to-back road blowouts, Michigan returned home and seemed to spot Indiana the first quarter in rainy, windy conditions. Michigan trailed 7–0, enduring a sluggish start with two straight three-and-outs, but responded by scoring on their next eight drives en route to defeating the Hoosiers 52–7. The defense came up with four turnovers and four sacks.

"They're fighters," Harbaugh said of Indiana. "They take their swings. Every year we play them, they're so well-prepared and ready to roll, and this was no different."

McCarthy threw for 222 yards and had three touchdowns, one each to Wilson and Morgan, but the most spectacular was a 54-yarder to Loveland. On third-and-10, McCarthy, under pressure, rolled right and appeared to be running for the first down when he pointed to Loveland down the sideline. "I was able to escape the pocket, then it was two-on-one with that defender and me and Colston," McCarthy said. "I told [Colston] go up field, so [the defender]'s got to pick his poison, and he picked the wrong one."

Backup quarterback Jack Tuttle also had a touchdown throw to Karmello English. Corum rushed for two scores, and Edwards had one. Rod Moore and Sabb each had an interception and Barrett and Graham each had a fumble recovery. While Harbaugh raved about the Hoosiers' fight, it was clear he was more impressed by what his Wolverines had put on display.

"We're fighters too, and I think that's what it says about the team," Harbaugh said. "It was a real calm, real understanding that, okay, when we get punched in the mouth, we're going to respond. That's what's going to happen. Everybody has that kind of faith in the leadership of our team, the character of our team. And there's a devotion to the fundamentals of Michigan football, and we just go to work responding, and that's the best strategy you can do. That's what we lean back on."

The Wolverines found ways to respond, but the success they'd found through the first seven games came from leaning on each other. That was a theme that would play out over the course of the season.

– 6 –

IN-STATE RIVAL, OFF-FIELD DRAMA

IT WAS TIME for the annual in-state rivalry game against Michigan State, the first time the two would play under the lights at Spartan Stadium. Not only was it a matchup of No. 2 and unbeaten Michigan against the struggling Spartans, winless after three games in the Big Ten under interim coach Harlon Barnett, but it was their first meeting since the postgame incident in the Michigan Stadium tunnel a year earlier after the Wolverines' 29–7 win. Video from an altercation involving MSU players and Michigan players Gemon Green and Ja'Den McBurrows quickly circulated after the game. Green and McBurrows had left the field while their teammates celebrated and walked up the tunnel with Michigan State players. Eight Michigan State players were eventually suspended, with seven charged, after Green and McBurrows suffered injuries.

Michigan players insisted Monday of game week while talking to reporters that the incident wouldn't be motivation for them heading into the upcoming game. Corum said the Wolverines were not talking about what happened and certainly weren't feeding off it during their preparations for this meeting in which they had been installed by oddsmakers as three-touchdown-plus favorites.

"We're just treating the game like the rivalry it is," Corum said. "We're not really focused on what happened last year. We're gonna go in there—well, first, we're going to handle business during the week, so we're gonna watch a lot of film—but Saturday, we'll go in there and handle business like always, like we have the past couple games. We're not going to hold a grudge on what happened last year. Always keep it in the back of the mind, but we're not going there being, 'Oh, we're going to rough them up,' or anything like that.... That's part of the past. We're going to go in there, handle business, and come out victorious."

Jaylen Harrell said it would be a mistake to allow the 2022 aftermath to be used as motivation. This Michigan team was on its own mission, and the game at Spartan Stadium wasn't going to change the history of the previous season. Their goal was about notching another win and keeping the Paul Bunyan Trophy in Ann Arbor.

"Obviously, it's a big game," Harrell said. "What happened [last year], we can't let our emotions get the best of us. Keep the main thing the main thing. We've got to handle business throughout the week [and] prepare. Not let it get to us."

Harbaugh wasn't interested in discussing the incident, either. That seemed so long ago to him and then cited what McCarthy had said about a "goldfish mentality," a reference to one of Harbaugh's favorite shows, *Ted Lasso*. For Harbaugh, it was all about the usual Michigan–Michigan State cliches, the ones that surface annually about playing for a state championship, throwing out the record books, and expecting a heck of a game.

Harbaugh wanted to use his time not to talk about the Spartans but to get McCarthy's name out in the Heisman Trophy mix. Michigan had never been known to campaign for Heisman Trophy consideration, with notebooks sent to voters or billboards or bobbleheads, and still had Desmond Howard and Charles Woodson win Heismans in 1991 and 1997, respectively. Harbaugh, who had already set the stage back in July at Big Ten media days, calling McCarthy a "once-in-a-generation quarterback," began to make an obvious push for the junior and didn't mince words.

"J.J has shown to be on path to be the best quarterback in Michigan history," Harbaugh said. "The statistics, I'm sure, speak to that."

McCarthy was 19–1 as Michigan's starter and, heading into the MSU game, he was one of the nation's most efficient passers, having completed 78.1 percent of his throws for 1,512 yards and 14 touchdowns—his three interceptions had all occurred in the third game of the season against Bowling Green. He also had proven to be a threat in the run game and had three rushing touchdowns. A few weeks earlier, Harbaugh mentioned that there are a lot of great college quarterbacks, "but I think he's the best one." At that point, Michigan had scored on 130 of the 213 drives (61 percent) that McCarthy had led during his career, 96 of those for touchdowns.

"It's really remarkable," Harbaugh said. "There's no statistic that demonstrates the quality of quarterback play more than that statistic in my mind. I think going forward, J.J. will be the quarterback that all future quarterbacks are compared to."

It wasn't like McCarthy was unknown nationally, but with Michigan's offense, he wasn't going to put up the kind of big numbers other Heisman contenders would (like USC quarterback Caleb Williams, the 2022 Heisman Trophy winner). There would be time for McCarthy to turn heads nationally, and Saturday night at Michigan State would be a good place to start.

Corum, meanwhile, took his leadership role as a co-captain seriously. Potentially being voted a captain was among the reasons he wanted to return for another season, and in that role, he thrived. After Tuesday's practice, he addressed the Wolverines with "wise words." That was something Harbaugh had introduced years earlier. Other teams had versions of this type of session, an opportunity for players and coaches to speak to the team, typically after a practice, but this is how it was referred to among the Michigan players. Corum found it important to remind the team not to think about the tunnel incident the year before.

"He was just saying, try not to make it too big," Barrett said of Corum's wise words. "We all know the hype of the rivalry, the hype of everything that's been going on, and just try not to make the scene too big. Be where your feet are and just prepare the same way. We try not to treat any team differently, any opponent differently or change the way we prepare or our business based on who we're playing. He basically said, handle your business and keep it pushing."

"[He] said it can be in the back of our heads, but we're not going to go out there trying to have any revenge," center Drake Nugent said. "We just have to play football and get out of there with a dub."

Nugent was at Stanford and transferred to Michigan after the 2022 season, so he wasn't at Michigan Stadium when the tunnel incident occurred. While he didn't know much about that situation, he had seen photos from previous Michigan–Michigan State games. This would be his first time playing in the game, and he knew one thing—you've got to bring home Paul. "I always remember the pictures I'd see on the Internet of whichever team won with the helmet on Paul running out of the tunnel," he said. "I don't know why, but I just love that image. We're going to get their best shot.... I've had the opportunity to be on the flip side of this at Stanford the past few years with rivalry games and playing against teams that were favored. You just can't give them that satisfaction, you can't overlook them. Just like any other week, you just gotta take it one week at a time, keep the preparation and focus high."

There was no way the players or coaches could have known it at that moment, but their season was about to face enormous upheaval, scrutiny, criticism, and the biggest challenge to their leadership.

On Thursday, two days before the Michigan–Michigan State game, Yahoo Sports reporters Ross Dellenger and Dan Wetzel reported that the NCAA had begun an investigation of the Michigan football program for allegedly violating rules that prohibit in-person scouting of future opponents. The allegation pertained to NCAA Bylaw 11.6.1: "Off-campus, in-person scouting of future opponents [in the same season] is prohibited." The NCAA does, however, allow staff members to scout future opponents "in the same event at the same site," per Bylaw 11.6.1.1.

The NCAA informed the Big Ten Conference of the investigation, and the conference issued a statement on Thursday after the Yahoo story broke:

> Late Wednesday afternoon, the Big Ten Conference and University of Michigan were notified by the NCAA that the NCAA was investigating allegations of sign stealing by the University of Michigan football program. The Big Ten Conference has notified Michigan State University and future opponents. The Big Ten Conference considers the integrity of competition to be of utmost importance and will continue to monitor the investigation. The Conference will have no further comment at this time.

It was unclear how this would affect Michigan, already involved in an NCAA violation mostly relating to impermissible recruiting visits during an COVID-19 dead period in 2021 and Harbaugh potentially facing a Level I violation, the NCAA's most severe, for allegedly misleading investigators.

Teams scout to prepare for upcoming opponents, but the question, according to sources who spoke to Yahoo, was whether Michigan had a staff member or members attend games of future opponents. Scouting enhances the prospects of sign-stealing, which also is not illegal unless scouting video was obtained improperly, such as using video or electronic equipment to share information among the coaches. According to the Yahoo report, two of Michigan's opponents said they became aware Michigan knew their play signs. It was unclear which programs were involved, but this shined a different light on Rutgers coach Greg Schiano's cryptic halftime comment during an on-field interview, when he said, "There are some things going on that aren't right."

Harbaugh, in a statement Thursday, said he and his staff were cooperating with the investigation:

> I do not have any knowledge or information regarding the University of Michigan football program illegally stealing signals, nor have I directed any staff member or others to participate in an off-campus scouting assignment. I have no awareness of anyone on our staff having done that or having directed that action. I do not condone or tolerate anyone doing anything illegal or against NCAA rule. No matter what program or organization that I have led throughout my career, my instructions and awareness of how we scout opponents have always been firmly within the rules.

Among the immediate reactions to the report of these allegations was that this likely would slow any progress made on a contract extension for the 59-year-old Harbaugh and possibly put contract talks on hold. It would be interesting to see how this could affect Harbaugh, considering that NCAA Bylaw 11.1.1.1, "Responsibility of Head Coach," could factor into the investigation. The bylaw, tweaked at the start of 2023, puts the onus on the head coach for all violations. "An institution's head coach shall be held responsible for the head coach's actions and the actions of all institutional staff members who report, directly or indirectly, to the head coach," the bylaw reads. This meant Harbaugh could be held accountable for any violations anyone on his staff had made if proven by the NCAA. This, on top of the other unresolved NCAA investigation, was hardly uplifting for a program in pursuit of a national title and about to play its in-state rival.

Michigan State, meanwhile, was attempting to navigate this breaking news since the Spartans were about to host the Wolverines in two days. Michigan State interim coach Harlon Barnett said he got a call Wednesday night from athletics director Alan Haller, who had spoken to officials from the Big Ten after the conference was notified by the NCAA of the investigation into Michigan. MSU officials reportedly approached the Big Ten and indicated it was considering not playing the game against Michigan, according to a sourced report in The Athletic. MSU cited concerns regarding the health and safety of its players, the implication being that if Michigan knew the Michigan State play calls ahead of time, the Spartans players wouldn't have as much time to react and could be injured. Michigan State eventually told the Big Ten the game would go on as scheduled.

Barnett would later confirm he was asked whether the Spartans should play. "At one time, somebody did mention possibly not playing the game," he admitted. "But I'm like, 'Let's play the game.' It don't get you until it gets you. Just remember that."

Michigan State interim president Teresa Woodruff issued a statement that never mentioned Michigan but made her point clear:

> As we look forward to the football game this Saturday, we are chagrined by the news of the NCAA investigation and we echo the Big Ten Conference's commitment to integrity. The allegations are concerning but will be handled through the NCAA's processes. MSU has no further

comment on that matter. The university is focused on supporting our own team and preparing campus for a safe game-day environment.

This was clearly a story that was picking up steam, certainly locally, but the national outlets were taking the lead. On Friday, there was more news out of Ann Arbor. Michigan football staff member Connor Stalions, an analyst for the program and a longtime, diehard Michigan fan who grew up in nearby Lake Orion before attending the Naval Academy, was suspended with pay by Manuel, the Michigan athletics director. Stalions had been identified in an ESPN.com report earlier that day as a "person of interest" in the newly opened NCAA investigation and was suspended by Manuel pending the conclusion of the investigation. The NCAA had requested computer records from Stalions, according to the ESPN report. He immediately scrubbed his social media accounts. According to his Twitter/X bio, he was a 2017 graduate of the U.S. Naval Academy and a 2013 graduate of Lake Orion High School. According to the University of Michigan's 2022 salary disclosure, Stalions, listed as "administrative assistant athletics," made $55,000. He was a volunteer assistant coach at Michigan beginning in 2015.

There was still a game to be played Saturday night at Spartan Stadium, and the Spartans quickly showed their adjustment on offense in light of the allegations against Michigan. Instead of using hand and sign signals, quarterback Katin Houser went to the sideline between each play to get the call directly from a backup quarterback. Barnett later said the Spartans had implemented that technique against other Big Ten teams who have had success stealing signs during games, which is not illegal.

Michigan State running back Nathan Carter later indicated the Spartans had prepared during their week of practice to huddle against the Wolverines. "I wouldn't say it was that big of an adjustment," he said. "We practiced huddling, going off of signals throughout the week. We knew going into the week that we were going to huddle a little bit, just to slow the game down for us as an offense, trying to control the game a little bit from that aspect. I wouldn't say that was a big change for us."

For the Spartans, there wasn't much remarkable about the game for them. They were never expected to be a factor in the game, and they weren't, as Michigan dominated in a 49–0 thrashing, after a blazing start with scores on four of five first-half possessions. The fans didn't even troll Michigan much during the game, even in light of the news of the NCAA investigation. At one point, Roman Wilson was sitting with teammates on the sideline, discussing the game plan with an assistant coach when he looked up and placed his hands around his eyes like he was holding binoculars. Wilson was looking at the one MSU fan who kept drawing their attention with his fake binoculars—a reference to Stalions. The players said after Wilson did that, the fan left and never returned.

On the heels of Harbaugh gushing about McCarthy's prowess as a quarterback, the junior went 21-of-27 for 287 yards and four touchdowns, including three to his tight ends. Colston Loveland caught two and AJ Barner one, and Wilson had a 25-yard touchdown reception. Corum and backup quarterback Alex Orji each scored on short runs. But there were a couple highlights from the secondary, the first from Mike Sainristil, who scored his second pick-six of the season, this time taking the interception 72 yards for the score with 9:49 left in the third quarter to build a 35–0 lead. When Sainristil reached the end zone, he put his hands on his hips and slightly tilted his head to the right in homage to the coveted Paul Bunyan Trophy. In the fourth quarter, McBurrows, who had been injured in the tunnel incident a year earlier and did not play that season, had an interception that essentially sealed the shutout. The Michigan sideline was overjoyed by his moment.

"All week he was talking about different things. He mentioned what happened last year a couple different times," Sainristil said of McBurrows. "But coaches and us as players, we told him, 'Man, when you get your chance, just go out there and make plays. Don't make no moment too big.' I'm so happy with how he played."

With the win, Michigan got to keep Paul. The trophy was born in 1953, the idea of then Michigan governor G. Mennen Williams, as a prize for the winner of the Michigan–Michigan State game. It features a four-foot-tall statue of mythical Paul Bunyan standing astride an axe, his hands on his hips with the slight head tilt. Former Michigan coach Lloyd Carr often referred to it as the "ugliest trophy in college football." The statue sits atop a five-foot base, and largely because of its size, it was long considered a locker room trophy and was celebrated by the winning team in its locker room. That changed in 2008 at Michigan Stadium when the then Michigan State coach, Mark Dantonio, and the Spartans snapped a six-game losing streak to the Wolverines and took Paul Bunyan off the stand and paraded around the stadium with an MSU helmet on his head. Ever since, it has been a stadium trophy, and it was no different after Michigan's 49–0 victory. Sainristil ran around with Paul, as the players lovingly refer to him, wearing maize pants and a blue Block M hat. A Michigan helmet eventually was added, and the Wolverines celebrated the win with their fans and Paul.

"We really had a single mindset on getting prepared and beating State," Harbaugh said after the game. "Pretty much if anybody around the building wanted to talk about anything else, they didn't want to. They wanted to just talk about the game preparation, practice, and get ready to play and execute. And I thought they played their best. Got a little saying around here that says, 'What you do speaks so loudly, can't even hear what you're saying.' So I thought our guys did a tremendous job just taking it one play at a time, and they were a real buzzsaw. Just played really, really great football."

Harbaugh was asked multiple questions about the latest NCAA investigation, and he referred each time to his statement issued two days earlier. "It's a heck of a group, and I just congratulate them," he said. "Their focus was laser-like. Staying strong, focused, on a mission."

To this point, Michigan had won 20 straight Big Ten games and was 21–1 over its last two seasons. With two NCAA investigations now ongoing, did he feel like perhaps Michigan had a target on its back? "Yeah, I think success does that to people who don't like to see people be successful," Harbaugh said. "There's a target? Yeah, I mean, everybody's pointed that out from the beginning of the season. But our guys are just very focused and just go about their business. Wake up, take care of business today, get the guys back to Ann Arbor, wake up tomorrow, and take care of business again."

But having that target is almost relished by athletes and teams. "It's just the first rule of being a champion—don't let up," he said.

McCarthy said Harbaugh had been upfront with the players about the latest investigation and told the players to maintain their focus. "Don't let it be a distraction," he recalled Harbaugh telling them. "Don't be a distraction."

And while Corum made such a point at the start of game-week preparations and even in his wise words session to encourage his teammates to not use the tunnel incident after the 2022 game as motivation, it was not a message that was fully embraced by each player. "I think it was really the thing that happened last year, the tunnel, that motivated us as well," Keegan said. "I know guys were like, 'Don't let it distract you,' things like that, and, 'We're over it.' No, we weren't over it. We wanted to come there and really beat down on 'em."

The bus ride from East Lansing to Ann Arbor takes a little more than an hour, and the defensive players were in one bus, the offensive players in another. The plan was for the offensive players to have the Paul Bunyan Trophy with them the first half hour, then, after a brief stop, the trophy would be transported to the defensive bus. Things started to get interesting on the offensive players' bus, where Harbaugh was.

"It was a little quiet," Keegan said. "All the guys were like, 'Man, why is it so quiet here? We just won 49–0.' So we ran up [to the front], and the bus had a microphone, so we started singing a bunch of songs."

First, the players, some using the lyrics found on their phones, sang along to "Ain't No Mountain High Enough," sung by Marvin Gaye and Tammi Terrell, then "Tennessee Whiskey" by Chris Stapleton, and "I Gotta Feeling" by The Black Eyed Peas. Emotions were sky high. Harbaugh then decided he had to sing to his favorite song by Gordon Lightfoot, "The Wreck of the Edmund Fitzgerald," a curious choice for a celebration tune, but it's one he long admired. A "real toe tapper" he once called it. He informed the players he was going to sing his favorite song of all-time.

"We're like, 'Oh, this is going to be a banger,'" Keegan said. "He grabs a mic, and he's singing a song just off the phone, and everybody is like, 'What? What song is this?' And he sang the whole song for like five minutes. And everybody is like, 'What song is this?'"

The players used an app on their phones that identifies music. The app was stumped, too.

"Shazam wasn't even reading it," Keegan said. "But we were just hyping him up, and he loved it. It came from his heart. It was a cool moment. When you're away in college football, there's always moments that are going to bring the team together more, and it's really cool."

It was these types of moments the players would rely on the rest of the season.

– 7 –

IMPROVEMENT WEEK

THE WOLVERINES headed into the week on a high having just shut out their in-state rival and with a certain buoyancy knowing they didn't have to prepare for a game on Saturday. They had played eight games, and their bodies were sore and needed some time to rest, as did their minds. They often talk about how much of a mental game football can be, so all in all, they were exhausted but feeling good about where the team was in terms of record and ranking. The players also liked the timing of this weekend off before November and the final, four-game, regular-season push that included their biggest challenges, at Penn State and at home against Ohio State. Harbaugh had already referred to the week before an off Saturday—often called in college football a "bye"—as "improvement week." This gave an opportunity to those who hadn't seen much playing time and younger players who needed more experience a chance to really be the focus of practices while the starters and key backups had a chance for a breather.

While their program was the subject of story after story with new findings about the illegal scouting allegations revolving around Stalions seemingly every day, the players seemed completely at ease in their own world. They were zoned in on football. McCarthy, after his outing against Michigan State, was now 20–1 over two seasons and had led the team to an 8–0 record at the break, and his name was getting more attention in the Heisman Trophy conversation.

"J.J. is just a great player," Harbaugh said after McCarthy threw four touchdowns against Michigan State. "I mean, that's just what it is."

McCarthy had never concerned himself with individual awards, and he wasn't about to start at this stage of his college career. Besides, he and his teammates were of one mind—national championship or bust. He admitted on that Monday that he had never thought about what it might be like going to New York for the Heisman presentation. "Because ever since I was young," McCarthy said, "I was just focused on putting rings on my finger, nothing other than that."

While he had built an impressive record as Michigan's starter, there was plenty to improve. The three interceptions in the Bowling Green game in Game 3 still gnawed at him. That game was humbling, he said and admitted that he went into that game feeling like he was going to have more touchdowns than incompletions. There's a difference between being confident and being bold. This was the latter. The three-interception game reminded him he must always respect every opponent and stay hungry. From that point on, McCarthy said he felt his mindset changed.

Since the Bowling Green game, McCarthy had made 101 pass attempts through five games without an interception. Those were hardly gaudy numbers by anyone's count, especially for a Heisman Trophy candidate. The Wolverines ranked sixth nationally in scoring offense, averaging 40.6 points per game, and had outscored its five Big Ten opponents 229–31. They had built large enough leads in most games that McCarthy was able to sit out the fourth quarters. The Big Ten opener against Rutgers was the exception, when he played the full game. But aside from that, he'd sat out for a little over seven quarters so far in the season. That's certainly a plus for a quarterback who intended to play another seven games, including a win in the national title game. And since it's never too early to ask a player about his playing future, he addressed whether he was already thinking about declaring for the NFL Draft after the season.

"I don't know right now. Nobody knows," he said. "Just so focused on the present moment, that never really comes in my head. That's going to come when it comes."

There was football happening inside the building, but outside, there were multiple national stories detailing what appeared to be large number of tickets purchased by Stalions to a growing number of games. Also that Monday, ESPN reported that Stalions purchased tickets in his own name for more than 30 games over the past three years at 11 different Big Ten schools. An opposing Big Ten school reportedly scanned in-stadium surveillance video from a game earlier in the season and found that an individual in the seat purchased by Stalions held his smartphone up and appeared to film the home team's sideline the entire game. The next day, the total swelled to 12 Big Ten schools with records of purchases made by Stalions, but he also bought tickets to the 2021 and 2022 SEC title games and the 2022 Oregon-Washington game. This reporting suggested a potential wide net of alleged illegal scouting and recording of games with tickets purchased in Stalions' name.

The players certainly weren't immune to questions about the intensifying scrutiny. After practice Tuesday night, offensive lineman Trente Jones said he wasn't concerned the latest NCAA investigation might diminish what the team had so far achieved. "It's more of another distraction that people come by and try and tarnish what we do," he said. "For me, specifically, I just try to prepare, get better each day, and take us to the next level."

There was no doubt they knew what was being reported. If they opened social media, it was there, if they turned on sports networks, it was there, too. How were they coping? Easy. "Knowing that it's us against the world," Jones said. "Knowing that all we need to get better to win to take the next step is us and that brotherhood."

These were the early steps of a team that would be galvanized dealing with so much out of the players' control. The "us against the world" motif would become bigger and more important. It wasn't exactly a unique approach, but for the Wolverines, that seemed the only way to not get sucked in and to use it as motivation to fulfill goals.

"We really don't pay attention to the outside distractions," safety Rod Moore said. "We just focus on what we have going on in here in this building as a team and what our goals are, and that's trying to get to the national championship and win the next game."

The players were never going to allow this to be a distraction. Perhaps their coach had more to concern himself with, but the players had wrapped themselves in an impenetrable cocoon of football. "We never really think of it as anything other than, Coach Harbaugh has to deal with something new once again," McCarthy said. "He does a great job of just keeping us focused on the main thing, which is winning football games."

The players used their time that week in various ways. Defensive back Josh Wallace decided to travel for the first time to Canada to shop, sightsee, and attend a Toronto Raptors game. Keegan opted to take time to do very little and was, he said, a "couch potato." He relaxed, watched football, and cleared his head to be ready for the most challenging portion of Michigan's schedule. Wilson said he did things he could not normally do during the season. He cleaned, took his dog to the park as often as possible, watched extra film, and also worked on his mental preparation for the rest of the regular season and what they hoped would be a lengthy postseason.

It was not nearly as relaxing for Harbaugh and his staff, or the Michigan athletics department, dealing with this new investigation while keeping the players locked in on the season and their goals.

The NCAA had arrived on campus that week to begin its investigation in earnest, but the organization is noted for its slow-moving process that never has any clear schedule and no real ending in sight. Michigan, as it said in its statements, was cooperating. The investigators were given access to cellphones and tablets from Michigan coaches and football staff to search for any sort of evidence—perhaps communication or collusion with Stalions. Acquiring data from phones and tablets is a typical first approach by NCAA investigators. The general process is that investigators obtain the data from those devices via mirroring, which projects the contents to another device. They also often request emails and laptops and, according to several reports, the NCAA had requested access to Stalions' laptop the day he was suspended by Michigan. The next step would be conducting initial interviews, likely the following week. The NCAA doesn't adjust its schedule for schools and teams, it's the other way around.

Meanwhile, more insight into how this investigation became reality was reported that week by the *Washington Post*, which had a lengthy story detailing how an outside investigative firm approached top NCAA officials on October 17 with information in the form of videos and various documents regarding the Michigan football program. A day later, the Big Ten was informed by the NCAA it had opened an investigation into the Michigan football program. The information had been obtained by the firm—the story never made clear who had hired the unnamed firm—through computer drives that could have been accessed by multiple Michigan coaches.

What was found, according to the *Post*'s accounting, suggested Stalions played a significant role in coordinating the alleged illegal sign-stealing scheme, but the investigative firm also indicated he likely was not acting alone. However, the firm did not find any evidence directly connecting Harbaugh to what Stalions had allegedly orchestrated, and it also didn't implicate any other coaches or staff members by name. The private investigators presented to the NCAA a detailed travel schedule for the remainder of the 2023 season, and it listed opponents' schedules and which games Stalions planned to have individuals attend and also how much money was budgeted for travel and tickets for scouting purposes. According to the *Post's* report, Ohio State games would be the most attended, with as many as eight scheduled. From the evidence the investigators shared with the newspaper, an estimated $15,000 was budgeted to spend on the scouting travel.

The outside firm shared with the NCAA photos the investigators believed were individuals scouting for Michigan while they were in the process of collecting video content that would be later uploaded to a computer drive maintained by Stalions. In the photos, the various individuals were in the seats purchased by Stalions and they could be seen aiming their cellphones at the sidelines presumably to shoot video of play calls as they were signaled in.

Off weeks during a football season tend to be quiet, slow news days, but this was clearly not the case at Michigan. And while there would be more allegations involving Stalions and ticket purchases at stadiums around the country, this became more of a challenge for the players, and for how the leadership from the captains would keep the team on track and steeled for whatever might be awaiting them on and off the field.

– 8 –

OPPORTUNITIES
FOR DISTRACTION

MICHIGAN players returned from the bye week after their win at Michigan State feeling refreshed, but it had been anything but a quiet break for Harbaugh. The night before he was to meet reporters for his weekly Monday news conference, the *Wall Street Journal* reported that in light of the recently launched NCAA investigation into the alleged illegal scouting/sign-stealing scheme, Michigan officials had "rescinded" a contract offer that would make Harbaugh the highest-paid coach in the Big Ten. Other reports suggested it was more of a "pause" in contract negotiations, and one described the offer as "temporarily withdrawn."

He would face questions at some point during his weekly Monday news conference about the upcoming game at home against Purdue, but the focus was on the *Journal's* report published the night before. He referenced his statement from October 19 that distanced himself from having any knowledge of the sign-stealing scheme while also saying he could not comment on an NCAA investigation. As far as the report that the contract was rescinded, Harbaugh responded flatly: "I wouldn't say that's accurate, no."

Harbaugh was then asked how these two NCAA investigations might affect his legacy. As he often did with questions he didn't want to answer, Harbaugh swerved and presented the message he wanted on the Monday of a game week, before addressing it. "Team is refreshed. I'm refreshed," he said. "Opportunity to spend time with the families after a pretty good week of practice. Last week, got some things done. And we're just onward. Onward mode. So I mean, to answer your question specifically, it's a one-track mind that I'm modeling, and I see it throughout the program."

They did have practices during the bye week, and because the players performed so well in them, Harbaugh gave them an extra day off. They rested and had a chance to take a break. But with no game the previous week, and more reports surfacing from national publications about Stalions and his alleged rampant ticket-buying spree for games involving future Michigan opponents, it was difficult to go a day without the program in the news. Harbaugh said he would not respond to any of it publicly, especially while busily preparing his team, still ranked No. 2 in the Associated Press poll. He mentioned several times about allowing the process, the investigation, to play out and that he would not engage in rampant speculation. When asked his strategy for his ability to maintain the one-track mindset he always talked about, he didn't hesitate. "I just channel my inner William Wallace," Harbaugh said. "That's the visual I think of to keep a one-track mind."

He was referring to the knight who famously led the Scots to victory against a larger English army in the Battle of Stirling Bridge in 1297. Wallace, who became a national hero, was a major figure in the First Scottish War of Independence and was the subject of the movie *Braveheart*, a favorite of Harbaugh's.

Michigan was readying for a night game against the Boilermakers who were 2–6 overall, 1–4 in the Big Ten. That wasn't exactly a fear-inducing way to kick off the final month of the regular-season for the Wolverines. Purdue was also riding a three-game losing streak under first-year head coach Ryan Walters heading into Michigan Stadium.

"The team is prepared to play 12:00 o'clock kickoffs. 3:30, 7:30, 9:00, whatever it is," Harbaugh said. "It's a team that understands and prepares, and whatever the situation—it's not always going to be 72 and zero humidity, either. It's gonna be cold, could be wet, could be hot, so they don't have to have everything set perfect. They're like field corn as opposed to being a houseplant. Nothing against houseplants. They have their other functions. They can be beautiful in the home. They can bring great, great beauty and value to a home. But the field corn, drop a seed in a crack on the sidewalk and it will burrow down and come up with any energy that it can find and then rise up in a stalk-like fashion and just start producing. I would say that's what our team is more like."

As for the players, they didn't seem remotely affected by the off-field drama. "This team is definitely focused on Purdue and Purdue only," Roman Wilson said. "This team is great. We don't get distracted. We just focus on ball."

Wilson shared a story the team heard in preseason camp heading into the season. It was not a new story to them. The veteran players had heard it during another season, but it defined how the players were avoiding getting wrapped up in the off-field noise. He was foggy on the details if it was Herbert or Harbaugh who had told the story this time, three months earlier, but it involved a storm and they were shown a photo of a buffalo, Wilson said, "just chilling in the storm." The takeaway was clear. "That's us," he said. "We're not running away from the storm. We're not scared of it. We're just chilling in it, and it's going to come through us and it's gonna pass by. That's the definition of this team."

The players also took matters into their own hands by disabling their social media accounts. There was no need to see all the negative headlines about Michigan, and, really, they didn't want to see any of the glowing praise for what they had already accomplished on the field.

"I deleted Twitter, because there's no point having it right now," Keegan said. "Just stay focused with the guys on the team, just keep grinding. People have got their opinions, they're welcome to have it, but as a team, as a leader, we're going to continue to be us. As a player that's been here a while, it's bothersome because we worked so hard to change this program and bring it back to where it's supposed to be. Everybody can make their allegations all they want, but the people who are in here, we know what we do, we know how we work, we know how we are as teammates. It's like a family here, so, it's, whatever, at this point."

Left tackle LaDarius Henderson, who transferred to Michigan from Arizona State before the 2023 season, made an appearance on Sirius XM radio during the week and was asked about the allegations and Harbaugh. "First off, we trust and believe in our head coach to be who he's always been, and we trust him and love him and believe that he's a man of integrity," Henderson said. "People might not believe it, but we're laser-focused on the task at hand, that being November. It hasn't been as big a thing in our building as it's probably been in everybody's living room the past few weeks. We're not gonna pause what we've got going on and pause our trajectory and steam to focus on noise that's coming from the outside."

That was how the Michigan players were handling the noise revolving around the allegations, but that did not reflect how everyone felt. There also was a news conference going on in West Lafayette, Indiana, that Monday afternoon as Walters, the first-year

Purdue coach, assessed his team and its preparations for Michigan. He praised the Wolverines' defense and remarked how McCarthy had obviously improved from the previous season. He was asked how Michigan's sign-stealing allegations might impact them in the game. "Impact them?" Walters said. "I'm not sure. My focus is on us and our team. Obviously, we're very aware of what the allegations are out there. We'll plan accordingly."

Late that Monday night, bombastic radio host Dan Dakich, a former college basketball player and coach, tweeted that he had spoken to a Big Ten coach and wrote that there was "word on the street" of video showing Stalions on the sideline of a team facing a future Michigan opponent "helping staff decipher Big 10 school signs. This shit is wild." Dakich then included a screengrab from the game of someone who appeared to be Stalions on the Central Michigan sideline wearing what the CMU assistants wore in a night game at Michigan State on September 1, the night before Michigan opened its 2023 season. The person alleged to be Stalions had a goatee, dark hair, and was wearing sunglasses, even though the game kicked off at 7:00 P.M.

The next day, other screengrabs of the person alleged to be Stalions on the CMU sideline surfaced and were widely circulated on social media. If it could be verified Stalions was that person on the sideline of a game against a future Michigan opponent—Michigan played Michigan State at Spartan Stadium on October 21—it would be the first clear-cut evidence that Stalions violated NCAA rule 11.6.1. That rule states: "Off-campus, in-person scouting of future opponents [in the same season] is prohibited, except as provided in Bylaws 11.6.1.1 and 11.6.1.2 [same event at the same site]." This rule was adopted in 1994. When originally contacted by the *Detroit News* on October 16, two weeks before the photos appeared, regarding the possibility Stalions was on the CMU sideline at MSU, a CMU spokesman said Stalions' name "was not on any sideline pass list, and the coaching staff was not aware he was on the sidelines." On

October 31, when multiple photos appeared, a CMU spokesman said the school was working to confirm if it was, indeed, Stalions. Central Michigan would eventually be visited by NCAA investigators and went the entire season without making a final assessment.

While the guy who was allegedly Stalions in disguise was the latest craziness involving Michigan in the college football world, that Tuesday night was also the first College Football Playoff rankings reveal. Michigan had been No. 2 in the Associated Press poll every week since the preseason poll was released, and at that point ranked No. 1 nationally in total defense (226.8 yards per game average) and scoring defense (5.9 points). McCarthy was No. 2 nationally in completion percentage (78.2 percent) and had become part of the Heisman Trophy conversation. But there were questions regarding how the CFP selection committee would view Michigan in light of this latest NCAA investigation. Those were answered during the reveal on ESPN as the Wolverines were No. 3 in the first rankings. CFP executive director Bill Hancock made clear Michigan remained in the playoff picture despite the latest NCAA investigation.

"You have to remember that these are allegations at this point and not facts, and so there's no substantive evidence that anything happened that might have affected the game," Hancock said. "All this committee does is evaluate what happens on the field during games." In fact, Hancock said, there was very little discussion of the investigation as the committee members evaluated Michigan.

Minter, the architect of the Wolverines' top-rated defense, met with reporters on Wednesday before practice and was asked about still photos that had appeared of him on the Michigan sideline with Stalions standing nearby in games from this season and 2022. "I wish we could speak on it, but we can't," he said. "It's fine. When you're at a job like this, there are going to be good days and bad days. You owe it to the players, you owe it to the coaches, you owe it to the people that are really important to you to do your job at a high level and keep working. That's what I've been able to do. Been able to try to stay focused. If we want the players to stay focused, we've got to stay focused. Trying to be that one-track mind for them and let the chips fall where they may."

There also was a story in The Athletic that day that featured an anonymous survey of 50 FBS college football coaches. From that group, 94 percent told Fox Sports' Bruce Feldman and The Athletic's Max Olsen that if the illegal scouting accusations proved to be true, Michigan should be punished. One coach told them Harbaugh should lose his job if the allegations wind up being true, and 70 percent polled said that Harbaugh lacked plausible deniability.

"I'm not going to speak to the speculation of what's happened here," Minter said when asked about this reaction from his coaching peers. "It is what it is. It's all speculation. Not going to speak on it."

Tight ends coach Grant Newsome, who also spoke to reporters on Wednesday, wouldn't comment on the survey, either. He took a page out of Harbaugh's book and changed course to discuss the team. "I think our team is incredible in the way they prepare, the talent they have, what they've put on tape every single week," Newsome said. "The stuff is going to play out how it plays out, and that's not something I'm going to speculate on. Just couldn't be more proud of our guys and what they put on the field every single week. I hope people can see that and appreciate just truly how good this team is."

A regularly scheduled conference call with Big Ten commissioner Tony Petitti and all of the Big Ten football coaches was held on Wednesday. This was not unusual. These typically are in-season meetings for the coaches to discuss any sort of conference business. ESPN's Pete Thamel was told by multiple sources that after a half hour, Harbaugh left the call so the remaining 13 coaches could speak freely about the NCAA investigation at Michigan and the illegal scouting and sign-stealing allegations. They spent an hour on the call, and the coaches were, reportedly, irate.

The next day, Nebraska coach Matt Rhule appeared on Andy Staples' podcast and shared that the call was the first opportunity for coaches to meet with Petitti to discuss the investigation at Michigan. "I think it was a chance for everybody just to kind of talk about how they felt, how they were impacted," he said in the interview. "I think a lot of people's lives, livelihoods, jobs, their seasons, players, players' health, all kinds of things, have been impacted by this."

Petitti spoke with Big Ten athletics directors during a conference call on Thursday afternoon after Manuel excused himself from the conversation. It was another opportunity for the commissioner to hear what the other programs thought on this matter, but he made no final decision regarding Michigan. He told the athletics directors he planned to meet with Big Ten school presidents and with Michigan officials.

That evening during his weekly radio show, Purdue's head coach Ryan Walters became the first coach to go on the record with the most pointed comments to date about Michigan and created a stir as his Boilermakers were getting ready to travel to No. 2 Michigan. Walters had been informed that Stalions bought tickets to six games at Purdue's Ross-Ade Stadium the last two seasons, including four games in 2023, as reported by ESPN. "It's unfortunate," he told radio host Tim Newton, who had asked about the Boilermakers' preparations for the Wolverines in light of the allegations. "What's crazy is they aren't allegations. It happened. There's video evidence. There's ticket purchases and sales that you can track back. We know for a fact that they were at a number of our games."

Armed with that information, Walters said he and his staff were making appropriate adjustments for this game. "We've had to teach our guys a new language in terms of some signals, and we'll operate differently offensively," Walters said. "You might see us in the huddle for the first time this season."

Petitti was scheduled to meet with University of Michigan president Santa Ono, who had gained significant popularity among Michigan fans because of his clear interest in athletics, particularly football and his support of Harbaugh, on campus Friday. Before that meeting, however, Ono sent Petitti an email cautioning the commissioner to not take lightly Michigan's side of this story, which had become contentious on so many levels. Ono wrote in the email that in situations like this, when all the facts are unknown, it is important that investigations are conducted fairly. Ono continued:

> None of us wants to be in this situation. The University of Michigan takes its compliance obligations seriously. We are committed to ethics, integrity, and fair play. It is at our core and always will be. And that is why I am so deeply concerned about the allegations. We are fully cooperating with the NCAA in its investigation, as it seeks to separate the facts from irresponsible speculation seen in much of the public and social media discourse. It's precisely at these times—when all key facts are not known but others are all too comfortable offering strongly held opinion—that it is essential for everyone to ensure that investigations are conducted fairly and that conclusions are based on what actually happened. The reputation and livelihoods of coaches, students, and programs cannot be sacrificed in a rush to judgment, no matter how many and how loudly people protest otherwise. Due process matters. We, as would any other member of the Big 10, deserve nothing less. Our students, our coaches, our program—all are entitled to a fair, deliberate, thoughtful process. We are aware that other representatives of the Big 10 are demanding that you take action now, before any meaningful investigation and full

consideration of all the evidence. That is not something our conference rules permit. And we both know it is not what any other member would want if allegations were raised against their people or programs.

The Big 10 has not informed us of any investigation of its own, as would be required under conference rules. And, to be clear, oral updates from NCAA enforcement staff do not and cannot constitute evidence, nor do we think the NCAA would ever intend for an oral update to be given that meaning or weight. The best course of action, the one far more likely to ascertain the facts, is to await the results of the NCAA investigation. But if you refuse to let the NCAA investigative process play out, the Big 10 may not take any action against the University or its players or coaches without commencing its own investigation and offering us the opportunity to provide our position. That is not just required by our conference rules; it is a matter of basic fairness.

When the contents of Ono's letter reached the public Saturday morning, he was hailed for his strong, proactive approach. But would it sway Petitti, who had the "exclusive authority," according to the the Big Ten's sportsmanship policy, to determine, using any evidence deemed relevant, if an "offensive action" has been committed. What the policy considered "standard" disciplinary action could yield no more than a two-game suspension and/or a fine up to $10,000. According to 10.1.2 of the policy, each institution is obligated to cooperate with the commissioner during the course of the investigation into whether an "offensive action" took place. Not cooperating is punishable. There also is a category for "major disciplinary action" that exceeds the up-to-two-game suspension and must be approved by the Joint Group Executive Committee (JGEC). The JGEC may approve, deny, or lessen the proposed penalty but not add to it. The committee is to act "as expeditiously" as possible. There is no appeal.

There was no update after Ono's meeting with Petitti on Friday, no sense whether he would, after hearing from coaches, athletics directors, and now Ono, take action against the football program and Harbaugh. But it was clear by the release of Ono's letter that Michigan officials wanted the fan base to be certain they were not sitting back and simply taking the punches.

As had been the case since this investigation was confirmed only two weeks earlier, there seemed to be no quiet moments, considering the headlines that had been generated revolving around Michigan football. The day before Michigan's game against Purdue was no different. Stalions, at the heart of the investigation, had been suspended with pay on October 20. According to his personnel file later released by Michigan, Stalions was informed on November 1 in a communication from Michigan human resources representative Tiffany Raymond of a disciplinary review meeting scheduled for the next day. "This conference is to discuss your failure to cooperate in a University of Michigan and NCAA investigation," Raymond wrote to Stalions. "Please be advised that termination of employment may result from this conference."

Nothing from the day of the disciplinary review conference was documented in his personnel file. The next day, Friday, November 3, the same day Petitti met with Ono, Stalions resigned.

"As we informed you earlier, Connor Stallions [sic] decided earlier today to resign from the University of Michigan," Stalions' attorney Brad Beckworth wrote to the university in an email sent at 7:57 P.M., Friday night, that appeared in his personnel file. "Connor has authorized us to send this email on his behalf to formally confirm his earlier decision to resign. Connor believes the recent stories regarding his time with the University of Michigan have created a distraction for the team and hopes that his resignation will help the team and coaching staff focus on tomorrow's game and the remainder of the season."

Stalions also issued a statement to The Athletic that night: "I am extremely grateful for the opportunity I've had to work with the incredible student-athletes, Coach Harbaugh, and the other coaches that have been a part of the Michigan football family during my tenure," Stalions wrote. "I do not want to be a distraction from what I hope to be a championship run for the team, and I will continue to cheer them on."

The opportunity for distraction didn't end, despite Stalions' resignation. On Saturday, hours before Michigan would kick off against Purdue at Michigan Stadium, Michigan received a notice of potential disciplinary action from the Big Ten, suggesting that Petitti was more swayed by the coaches and athletics directors than by Ono. Lawyers representing Michigan and those representing Harbaugh would have only a few days to file a response.

Finally, after two weeks, there was football to be played, and the Wolverines were back on the field. They didn't seem to miss a step, especially Corum, who scored three touchdowns in a 41–13 victory over the Boilermakers to improve to 9–0. The touchdowns moved Corum into a tie for second in career rushing scores with Tyrone Wheatley at 47, only nine away from breaking Anthony Thomas' program record of 55. The Wolverines build a 20–0 lead in the first half before allowing two field goals before halftime. With just more than three minutes left in the third quarter, freshman receiver Semaj Morgan made a dynamic, 44-yard run to build a 27–6 lead. Morgan is gifted with speed, which was on display during his big-gain play.

"He's electric," Harbaugh said after the game. "Ball in his hands, it's got a chance to go the distance. He's just strong. Not huge in stature. It's not the size of the dog in the fight but the size of the fight in the dog. The guys love him. It's a spark the way he competes."

Michigan would score twice more on runs from Corum and Edwards before allowing Purdue's only touchdown with 18 seconds left.

After the game, the handshake between Harbaugh and Walters was greatly anticipated. The men never paused and blew past each other with the barest hint of a handshake. "Typical postgame handshake," Harbaugh said in his postgame news conference.

"I shook his hand and came to the locker room," Walters said. Once Walters made it to the postgame interview room, he doubled down on the comments he had made about Michigan on the radio show Thursday night. "Just calling a spade a spade, really, in terms of advantages or disadvantages," he said. "Just stating what happened."

He revealed that he did not believe his comments on the radio show would go viral. "I didn't think so," he said. "Again, I usually tell the truth, it's not like a big deal, you know what I mean? But, yeah, I would say that I made breakfast Friday morning and got a cup of coffee and turned on *SportsCenter*, and I was on the ticker. That was like an 'Oh, okay' moment. But again, I'm not shy about speaking truth, and if I could do it over again, I'd say the same thing."

Meanwhile, at Harbaugh's news conference, he was asked about the commissioner's meeting with Ono the day before and said that, while he appreciated the question, he was not permitted to speak about it. "Not talking about him," Harbaugh said. "Really want to talk about the game. The guys were such stalwarts. The comments keep coming about why they're good, how they're good. They're just good. If you know football and you watch our guys play—and I've said it before— there's 20, 22, 23 guys that will be playing on Sundays next year. It's just really good players. If you know football, just watch the game. Turn on the tape. That's why they're so good. They're good at it."

Warde Manuel regularly attended Harbaugh's postgame news conferences, and he also declined to comment or even offer a timeline for when a response might come from Petitti. "I have nothing to say," he said multiple times to reporters. "I'm here to see Jim and celebrate this victory."

With an important final stretch ahead in the East Division, with a game the next week at Penn State and then at Maryland before returning home to face Ohio State, and the Wolverines eyeing a third-straight Big Ten championship, the players were asked if they felt they had something extra to prove in light of the allegations. "We don't gotta prove nothing," Donovan Edwards said. "All we got to do is just do what we do, and that's just play ball, that's love each other, that's play for each other. It's nothing that we have to prove. If there's anything that we have to prove is to ourselves. We don't have to prove nothing to nobody. To be honest, we don't care what outside people say. All we care about is what people in Schembechler Hall say, and that's the people that are there on a day-to-day basis. That's the people who actually know what's going on inside of Michigan football. We don't gotta prove nothing to nobody. Just keep doing what we're doing as that's going to take us very far, as it has so far."

There were a lot of positives on the field, although McCarthy felt he wasn't at his best in terms of accuracy. But he noted that it wasn't a huge issue, considering the offense could still score 41 points. He was 24-of-37 for 335 yards with no touchdowns or interceptions. There were dropped passes among the incompletions, but he also took three sacks, which was more of an issue than his accuracy. Roman Wilson had a big day with 143 yards on nine catches. On defense, cornerback Will Johnson got his second interception of the season thanks in large part to defensive end Jaylen Harrell's pressure on Purdue quarterback Hudson Card.

Minter's defense was stingy again when it mattered most. The Wolverines entered the game No. 1 nationally in red-zone defense and in the second quarter stopped Purdue at the Michigan 15-yard line and then the 14-yard line on back-to-back series, holding the Boilermakers to field goals. Both those field goals came off errors by Michigan, each giving Purdue its only starting field position in Michigan territory—both times at the 34-yard line. The Wolverines had a punt-return snafu when the ball hit off a Michigan player and was recovered by Purdue, and the Wolverines failed on fourth-and-1, turning the ball over to the Boilermakers.

The Michigan players were asked if they heard any trash-talking from Purdue players that involved the sign-stealing allegations. "I heard some fans yelling, but nah, I don't think anybody on the field really cared too much about it," linebacker Michael Barrett said with a laugh. "Heard some fans asking where our guy was at."

By their "guy," the fans obviously were referring to Stalions.

If the players were concerned there could be any type of long-term punishment against Michigan, things like vacating wins or a postseason ban, they weren't showing it. Sure, they heard some heckling from fans and assumed there would be more the next couple weekends on the road, but that's not something that breaks a team. They were buoyed by Ono sending the email to Petitti and laying out a case for Michigan to be treated fairly, and they felt good about his support, which Harbaugh said was "deeply appreciated."

"We just control what we can control," McCarthy said. "We know one thing's for sure, President Ono is the best president in the country and we absolutely love him. He's done many great things for us other than just making that statement."

But would that be enough? Now it was about Michigan's and Harbaugh's lawyers preparing responses to Big Ten commissioner Petitti and the notice of potential disciplinary action he issued. They would have to be persuasive in their arguments if Michigan hoped to avoid punishment. The next several days would be tense.

– 9 –

MICHIGAN'S FIRST
MAJOR TEST

HARBAUGH never behaved like he was feeling the heat, but he was definitely under fire from rival coaches and fans, not to mention the Big Ten. He threw some water on that when he began the Penn State game week full of enthusiasm after a visit from his friend, Ric Flair, the wildly popular professional wrestler and noted Michigan fan. The two had been friends since Harbaugh played for the Chicago Bears. Harbaugh's then teammate, Brad Muster, was a fan of Flair's, known as the "Nature Boy," and Harbaugh eagerly tagged along with him to an event in 1989. Harbaugh had never before been invited backstage to any kind of function or concert, but there he was with Muster meeting Flair. He said they became "instant friends." Harbaugh and Muster became part of the "hype squad" that night, grabbed a towel, and cheered on Flair for the first of many visits.

"He's one of a kind," Harbaugh said Monday before the Penn State game, "the best."

Flair had become, in some ways, Harbaugh's hype man, and his visit invigorated the coach. Harbaugh knew all about the angry Big

Ten coaches' conference call, the general feeling toward him and his program, and that there were loud demands for punishment from conference members. After the win over Purdue, he and Walters, who had come out strongly about Harbaugh and the allegations, had that notably frosty postgame handshake. While Harbaugh seemed enthused and charged by Flair's visit, he was asked if this specific spotlight on him was motivating. "Nobody wants criticism," Harbaugh said. "That's why I work so hard to do everything right both on and off the field. It's been that way for a long time, since I was 22 years old. If the criticism is directed to me and not towards my adolescent kids at home or the players on the football team, then I am okay with it."

Harbaugh and Michigan had no choice but to await whatever potential punishment Petitti and the Big Ten determined. He deflected a question about whether he cares about respect for him within the coaching profession, saying he appreciated the inquiry, but stated his position clearly. It might not have been planned this way, but Flair's presence was interesting timing. He was known in the WWE as the greatest heel in professional wrestling. A "heel" in pro wrestling terms means a *villain*. The Michigan players didn't believe they had been party to any wrongdoing, but they knew the perception was out there that they had benefited from illegal scouting. In other words, the perception was they had cheated. In the meantime, they had become, unwittingly, villains, and instead of running away from it, they embraced it.

"I know there's a lot of noise going on outside of the building," offensive lineman Zak Zinter said. "I haven't really paid too much attention to it. But if someone thinks we're the villain, I'm fine being the villain. Sometimes the villain wins and takes down the superhero. So, if that's going to be the case, let's be the villain and let's take them down. I'm fine with being the villain if that's how the media and everyone else sees it outside the building."

Harrell said the players had been unflappable. They were unmoved by the criticism. Yes, they had been hearing and reading about it, thanks in large part to social media, but they found it fairly easy to ignore. That's what villains do. It fuels them. "I guess it's an extra little chip," he said. "Whatever people have to say and outside crowd noise, we don't pay attention to it. Our main focus right now is to prepare this week and get ready to battle with Penn State."

Still, what was potentially brewing in terms of a Big Ten response regarding Michigan was definitely being taken seriously at Michigan. Later that Monday, Manuel, a member of the College Football Playoff selection committee, revealed he would not travel to Texas for the committee meeting while he focused on the upcoming decision from the Big Ten and would remain in Ann Arbor. "Attending to important matters regarding the ongoing investigation into our football program," Manuel said in the statement. "I look forward to being back in the room with my fellow committee members next week and every week through the end of this season."

This was not the first time a committee member had missed a meeting. Manuel, like any committee participant representing a school that's part of the CFP process, was recused when the committee discussed Michigan. Bill Hancock, the CFP's executive director, had insisted a week earlier after the release of the first rankings that Michigan remain in consideration for the playoff because nothing concrete had been revealed in terms of the allegations. And that was Hancock's key point. Allegations are not facts, and the CFP committee evaluates what teams do on the field, period. After the CFP rankings reveal Tuesday night ahead of the Penn State game, Michigan ranked No. 3 again. Hancock, in a post-rankings conference call with reporters, insisted for a second-straight week that the allegations regarding Michigan and the sign-stealing scheme did not come up during their discussions and deliberations.

The noise outside the program was loud, but there also was a lot of noise in the practice facility during the week. Teams preparing to go on the road to raucous stadiums like Penn State's Beaver Stadium typically turn up the music or recorded crowd noise during practice. This is really meant to prepare the offense to avoid being disrupted by a loud crowd, which can challenge communication and often causes false-start penalties. New speakers had been installed in the Al Glick Field House, Michigan's indoor practice facility, and they got a workout. McCarthy would later say that it was louder in Glick than in Beaver Stadium and joked he was worried he might lose his voice before leaving Ann Arbor.

From the standpoint of the coaches, they had said repeatedly that this team was easy to keep on track. This week seemed no different. Penn State was the second of the "States" Michigan had to defeat to keep their goals intact, and that was enough of a motivation. Hart, the Wolverines' running backs coach, said during a midweek meeting with reporters that it was easy for all of them to stay focused heading into the first of back-to-back road games. "Everybody knows what the end goal is," he said. "The players know who they are, the coaches know who we are. To me, it's one of those things we really don't even talk about it. Let's stay focused on the task at hand and control what you can control. That's all we can do. Control what you can control, and it'll go from there. I know these players are hungry. They're thirsty. They want a Big Ten championship; they want a national championship; and they know we gotta beat Penn State. That's all they're focused on right now. That's what we're focused on right now and care about."

A few hours after Hart spoke on Wednesday, November 8, Michigan officially submitted its response to the notice of potential disciplinary action that Petitti and the Big Ten had issued four days earlier before Michigan's game with Purdue. Lawyers for Michigan and Harbaugh had requested an additional 24 hours for their responses and made separate filings before 5:00 P.M. Michigan's lawyers filed a 10-page response and Harbaugh's lawyers an eight-page response. They had made their best efforts to defend Harbaugh and Michigan. In the university's response to the Big Ten, which was obtained by Yahoo Sports, it argued there was no threat to sportsmanship or competitive balance that would require suspending Harbaugh: "We are not aware of any evidence or allegation suggestion that violations are ongoing now that Stalions is no longer part of the football program," the university response said. "Absent such evidence, there is no discernible reason for…refusing to provide due process." The response also said the university was unaware of any instance when the sportsmanship policy "has ever been deployed as a backdoor way of holding an institution responsible for a rule violation that has not been established."

Thursday came and went with no response from the Big Ten.

Meanwhile, the players, fairly insulated from the latest details involving their coach, the Big Ten, its commissioner, the university president, and all of the characters playing a role in this tug of war, were not completely unaware. Their show of unity began to take shape this time as they started to appear at interviews and when leaving the football building in MICHIGAN VS. EVERYBODY sweatshirts and hats. Shortly after the gates opened for name, image, likeness (NIL) revenues in 2021, Valiant Management Group, which works with Michigan athletes on NIL, launched the "Michigan vs. Everybody" apparel with sales collected into a royalty pool and distributed equally among athletes who opted to participate in the program. There was what amounted to a re-release of the line the week leading up to the Penn State game, and sales were brisk. By the end of what would become an eventful weekend, more than $50,000 worth of "Michigan vs. Everybody" apparel would be sold, the money collected for Michigan athletes.

On Friday afternoon, the players were upbeat as they headed to the plane for the trip to State College to face Penn State, which featured the toughest defense they'd face to this point in the season. Many said it would be the first major test of the season for the Wolverines, and as a contender in the Big Ten East Division, this game carried plenty of weight. Most of the players boarded the charter plane wearing "Michigan vs. Everybody" gear. Harrell wore the sweatshirt, LaDarius Henderson wore the knit hat, while Barrett and Corum wore black long-sleeve shirts with the slogan in a slightly lighter shade of black.

They had no idea what drama awaited. Just moments before landing at University Park Airport in State College, at 3:54 P.M., Harbaugh, Manuel, the staff, and players turned on their phones. Harbaugh said someone reached over his shoulder to show him a phone screen with breaking news on social media that had posted eight minutes earlier while the Wolverines were making their descent into Happy Valley. Petitti had imposed a three-game suspension on Harbaugh for the final three regular-season games, beginning with the Penn State game the next day.

"We land, and in the air your phone's not on, so you're just getting ESPN reports, and we're like, 'What? What's going on?'" Michigan cornerback Josh Wallace told reporters at the NFL Combine in late February 2024. "And then we saw that Coach Harbaugh got pulled aside, and we were like, 'Oh, shoot, this is happening.'"

Manuel was outraged he had heard the news through social media and not from the Big Ten office. Once they deplaned, Harbaugh stood on the tarmac by the plane with Herbert, Manuel, and Manuel's chief of staff, Doug Gnodtke, trying to determine their next steps.

"We were all looking around like, 'Oh shoot, like this is crazy,'" receiver Cornelius Johnson said. "I've never really had something like that [happen], at least in my playing career. And that added to the fire of going out with our mindset, especially on the road, too, it's just that mindset that it's just us in there and that's all we need."

Petitti and the Big Ten said Harbaugh would not be allowed to be at the stadiums for the final three games, away at Penn State and Maryland, and at home in Michigan Stadium against Ohio State in the regular-season finale. Harbaugh could continue to oversee practices leading up to games.

The Big Ten, in announcing the suspension, said it was unmoved by Michigan's response to allegations of an elaborate sign-stealing scheme that the NCAA was investigating. In a 13-page letter to Manuel, the Big Ten said while there was no direct evidence linking Harbaugh to the alleged scheme involving Stalions, who had since resigned, Harbaugh deserved the punishment as the face of the program. Petitti said the decision was based on evidence received from the NCAA, which first began investigating the allegations in mid-October. The Big Ten also said it found no evidence that other programs were sharing information to decode Michigan's signs, "let alone a scheme of the size and scale like the one at issue here."

"The extensive information obtained by the conference has led me, in my capacity as conference commissioner, to conclude that the university violated the sportsmanship policy," Petitti said in the letter to Manuel. "That policy requires the commissioner to determine the appropriate discipline 'as expeditiously as possible.'"

Michigan then released a strongly worded statement and said it would seek an immediate court order, despite the fact it was Veteran's Day, a court holiday, to keep Harbaugh on the sideline at Penn State. The statement read, in part:

> Like all members of the Big Ten Conference, we are entitled to a fair, deliberate, and thoughtful process to determine the full set of facts before a judgment is rendered. Today's action by Commissioner Tony Petitti disregards the Conference's own handbook, violates the basic tenets of due process, and sets an untenable precedent of assessing

penalties before an investigation has been completed. We are dismayed by the Commissioner's rush to judgment when there is an ongoing NCAA investigation—one in which we are fully cooperating.

Commissioner Petitti's hasty action today suggests that this is more about reacting to pressure from other Conference members than a desire to apply rules fairly and impartially. By taking action at this hour, the Commissioner is personally inserting himself onto the sidelines and altering the level playing field that he is claiming to preserve. And doing so on Veteran's Day—a court holiday—to try to thwart the University from seeking immediate judicial relief is hardly a profile of impartiality. To ensure fairness in the process, we intend to seek a court order, together with coach Harbaugh, preventing this disciplinary action from taking effect.

Back in his room at the team hotel, defensive back Mike Sainristil, on his video blog, looked seriously into the camera and shared how he felt. "I ain't going to say too much, but it's more fuel to the fire," he said, referring to the Harbaugh suspension. "That's all it is. All we can do is go play for him."

A little more than an hour after they landed, the Michigan players took to the social media platform X to express themselves, with defensive tackle Kris Jenkins leading the way. Jenkins posted a simple message: "Bet." McCarthy then posted the same message, "Bet." Zak Zinter, Junior Colson, Michael Barrett, Trevor Keegan, Sainristil, Wallace: *Bet, Bet, Bet, Bet.* It seemed endless. Even former Wolverine and seven-time Super Bowl champion Tom Brady got in on the act and posted the same message, "Bet." Ono, the university president, would also post the message later that evening. There are a number of ways to interpret the meaning of "Bet," but in this context it was meant in defiance. Essentially, it meant, "Okay, let's go."

By Friday night, Michigan filed for a temporary restraining order in Washtenaw County's 22nd Circuit Court, which would prevent the Big Ten from imposing the suspension before arguments were heard if supported by the court. It wasn't immediately clear how soon the court would act. Although Friday was the observation of Veterans Day, a federal holiday, judges were available for what are considered emergency decisions. Michigan's statement alleged Petitti was announcing the decision on that day "to try to thwart the university from seeking immediate judicial relief."

In the university's response to the Big Ten, it argued there is no threat to sportsmanship or competitive balance that would require suspending Harbaugh. The response also said that the university is unaware of any instance when the sportsmanship policy "has ever been deployed as a backdoor way of holding an institution responsible for a rule violation that has not been established." Harbaugh's lawyers, in their letter, argued the Big Ten can't punish Harbaugh when there is no evidence that he committed the "offensive behavior." The letter was signed by lawyers Tom Mars (who was also representing Harbaugh in the other NCAA investigation) and Jeff Klein. They argued: "The Big Ten rules do not permit the commissioner to impose liability on Coach Harbaugh after being informed by the NCAA that it has found no evidence that he was in any way implicated in Connor Stalions' alleged misconduct. This finding is consistent with both Coach Harbaugh's statement immediately after this matter came to his attention and the statement released thereafter by Connor Stalions' lawyer."

A request for a temporary restraining order was submitted that night in a 219-page filing by lawyers for Harbaugh and the Michigan Board of Regents. They were not caught off guard by the commissioner's decision to suspend and evidently were prepared to file the request.

The next morning, game day, there was still no ruling on the temporary restraining order. Harbaugh did not board the team buses, but there was alternative transportation with a police escort ready if he got the signal he was cleared to coach. The players and staff always look serious when they exit the buses before the game, but there was a different vibe when they walked off toward the locker room. It was about two and a half hours before kickoff. They didn't have their head coach, and they had to summon their one-track-mind focus. Some of the Michigan fans who made the trip walked around with FREE HARBAUGH signs.

Less than an hour later at about 10:20 A.M., it was revealed that Judge Timothy Connors would not make a ruling on the temporary restraining order. Harbaugh would not be able to coach the Wolverines, and he wouldn't be allowed at the stadium. A hearing was set for the following Friday as Michigan and Harbaugh planned to fight for a preliminary injunction so that he could coach the final two games.

"We look forward to presenting our case next week where we intend to demonstrate that the Big Ten has not acted legally or fairly," Michigan said in a statement Saturday morning, about an hour before game time.

It didn't end there. Manuel, less than a half hour before kickoff, issued a fiery, lengthy statement that called out Petitti and the Big Ten. For Manuel, who generally didn't make himself available for media interviews and stayed mostly in the background, this was a bold response. He wrote:

> I want to make it clear at the outset of this statement that no one at the University of Michigan is happy to hear of the allegations and preliminary evidence that has come forth about in-person scouting and sign stealing by a member of

our football program. No one. We, like every institution in this country, preach and educate all of our student-athletes, coaches, and staff, to adhere to rules and ask questions if something is unclear.

However, no one here, and no one at other universities around this country, wants to be convicted and penalized without due process of a complete investigation and with significant harm to our student-athletes. This is a fundamental principle of our justice, NCAA and, until yesterday, our conference systems. Sadly, that is not what happened yesterday.

Yesterday, under the guise of the NCAA Rule regarding Head Coach Responsibility the Big Ten decided to penalize Coach Harbaugh without knowing all the facts, and I find that completely unethical, insulting to a well-established process within the NCAA, and an assault on the rights of everyone (especially in the Big Ten) to be judged by a fair and complete investigation. Not liking someone or another university or believing without any evidence that they knew or saying someone should have known without an investigation is not grounds to remove someone from their position before the NCAA process has reached a conclusion through a full NCAA investigative process.

All of the Head Coaches in the Big Ten (some who have been accused of actively participating in the trading of signals of opponents) and my Big Ten AD colleagues can rejoice today that someone was "held accountable," but they should be worried about the new standard of judgment (without complete investigation) that has been unleashed in this conference.

You may have removed him from our sidelines today, but Jim Harbaugh is our head football coach. We look forward to defending Jim's right to coach our football team at the hearing on Friday. He has instilled his pride, passion, and the team's belief in themselves to achieve greatness. I will continue to support Jim throughout this process, my coaches and staff, and especially our student-athletes as we continue to play this game and fight to win for Michigan and all who love us.

Manuel fielded a number of questions two months later about the team and Harbaugh and at one point revisited this situation at Penn State and his lengthy, angry response to Petitti and the Big Ten for suspending Harbaugh. Manuel said, ultimately, Petitti made a decision with which he disagreed, but that didn't alter their ability to work together. He called Petitti a "good person" and said although they were at odds on this Harbaugh decision, that didn't mean he didn't like him. Manuel was asked if he regretted the tone of the statement.

"I don't regret anything, I promise you that," Manuel said as he walked away. "Promise."

Despite the effort to obtain a temporary restraining order, and the statements from Michigan and Manuel, Harbaugh would have to watch his team, led by Moore as the acting head coach, on television from the team hotel. The night before the game, Harbaugh, who at that point believed he would be on the sideline, told the players to "play angry." It wasn't a message, Moore would later say, about vengeance, but about encouraging the players to do what they always do—play together, play fast, play physical.

The Wolverines would win the game 24–15, in the most Harbaugh of ways—with grit—as exemplified in the second half by 32 consecutive runs. McCarthy was not credited with a pass in the second half—there was a pass-interference call on the lone attempt—and the defense forced four three-and-outs, a turnover on downs, and a fumble while holding Penn State to 4-of-14 on third-down conversions. Both teams entered the game without having allowed a third-quarter point, but only Michigan would remain unscored upon in the third quarter through 10 games, increasing their margin to 117–0. The Wolverines snapped the Nittany Lions' third-quarter dominance with a field goal.

Moore's postgame television interview created a much-publicized stir and, as is the case these days, instantly became a social-media meme. Harbaugh would later say he was "five inches from the TV" as he watched Moore, his face sometimes contorted and his eyes filled with tears, give an expletive-riddled response to Fox Sports reporter Jenny Taft about leading the team to victory in those unusual circumstances. "I want to thank the Lord," Moore told Taft in the emotional interview. "I want to thank Coach Harbaugh. I fucking love you, man. Love the shit out of you, man. This is for you, for this university, the president, our AD. We got the best players, the best university, best alumni in the country. Love you guys. These fucking guys right here. These guys did it. I love you."

When he reached the postgame news conference, Moore was immediately asked about his emotional television interview. "I think it was all built up," he said. "Was thinking about our players and how hard they've worked through all this craziness and all the situations that's been going on, how hard they have worked and the realization of that coming to fruition and watching it come to fruition against a great football team. That football team is really good. Defensively, offensively, special teams, in all three phases, they're as elite as they come. For us to come in this environment and win was huge. Just thinking about Coach, man. Love that man with all my heart. Such a great person, great human, great coach. Just wanted to do it for him."

The Michigan players were determined to play angry. That's what Harbaugh had told them the night before. That's what he wanted their mindset to be, and that's what it was. After the win, McCarthy said he and several of his teammates communicated with their head coach via FaceTime.

"Obviously, everything that happened [Friday], we just wanted to use that as fuel and motivation," Keegan said. "We got a very hungry team, guys that just want to prove the haters wrong. They're gonna be hating on us, and we just want to prove them wrong. We wanted to do this for Coach Harbaugh, come in here and get a gritty win. Can't be more proud of the guys and everybody that we have in that locker room. The adversity that hit, we just punched it in the face."

It was a bizarre box score for McCarthy, but that was to be expected with a second half of all run plays. He was 7-of-8 for 60 yards and also had eight carries for 34 yards. Late in the game, he came off the field limping but played on. McCarthy, who would later say he was fine physically, said the performance at Penn State was proof of the Wolverines' ability to adapt to what the defense, this time led by Penn State's outstanding edge rusher Chop Robinson, gave them.

"With one of the best offensive lines in the country and obviously two of the best backs in the country, we just got to take what they give us," McCarthy said. "We adapted, we adjusted, and kept rolling."

The story of the game would be Corum and Michigan's commitment to the run, an adjustment made when it was clear in the first half that Penn State's defense, particularly Robinson, the dynamic edge rusher, was making life difficult for the Wolverines' offensive line and giving McCarthy little time. Michigan and Penn State entered the game ranked No. 1 and No. 2 in the country, respectively. The Nittany Lions were especially dominant against the run, holding teams to 60.3 yards per game, best in the nation. That didn't matter to Moore, who determined the only way to leave Happy Valley with a win was to run the ball and run it some more. And more. In his words, it was about *smash*, a word, a style of play he made popular the previous season to mean the Wolverines' ability to be physical in the run game from the backs to the offensive line.

"This was a tournament game for us, a playoff game for us, so we knew we had to do whatever we needed to do to win," Moore said. "It's been a crazy 24 hours, but at the same time our team is built for this, our staff is built for this. We're all built for it."

The Wolverines rushed for 227 yards against Penn State, and Corum scored two touchdowns, including a 30-yard run on the first play from scrimmage with 4:15 left in the game that gave Michigan a 24–9 lead. He had 145 yards on 26 carries, including a 44-yard run, and increased his rushing touchdown total for the season to 18.

While his performance was critical to the win, it was the appearance of Corum's face in the postgame interview that would wind up defining the season and this team. A close-up photo of Corum's face taken by Herbert would be widely circulated on social media. He had an eye-black strip stretched across his nose under his eyes, and blood-soaked, criss-crossed tape over the bridge of his nose. It was not the first time he had blood on the bridge of the nose, a result of the helmet rubbing a spot that had never completely healed. There was a smudge of blood above his right eye and blood seeped from the gash on his nose and trickled down the left side of his face. Some blood had gathered under his right eye. A few days later in Michigan's facility, the photo had become a framed poster with STALWART on top, then the score added to his eye black and SAVAGE WARRIOR at the bottom.

Several months later at the NFL Combine, Corum would tell *Pro Football Talk* that the win at Penn State convinced him the Wolverines had that extra something special that champions have.

"The game when I knew we were gonna win it all was Penn State," Corum said. "In the second half, we ran it 32 times straight without a pass. And once we established that, dang, we're physical, we're gritty. You run it 32 times straight, that's something serious. That's insane. That's the game I knew we were really special."

There were other moments in the game that convinced Corum that Michigan could win it all. The defense played a significant role, holding Penn State to 238 yards. The Nittany Lions' quarterback Drew Allar was 10-of-23 for 70 yards and took a sack by Harrell. Johnson shut things down, as well, and had two pass breakups. There was a signature defensive play late in the second quarter when Kaytron Allen ran 34 yards on the opening play of the Nittany Lions' final drive of the half and appeared to be going the distance. Allen, who is 5'11", 222 pounds, was run down with incredible athleticism at the Michigan 41-yard line by an unlikely tackler—6'3", 339-pound sophomore defensive tackle Kenneth Grant. A year earlier, Harbaugh had referred to Grant and fellow tackle Mason Graham as "gifts from the football Gods."

"I was up off my feet," Harbaugh said of watching Grant on television making the stop. "One of the best plays of the season, that play by Kenneth Grant. Maybe one of the best plays ever. It was a guardian-of-victory type of play. Kenneth was dominant in the game. He was the real tone-setter right from the first series. Only a sophomore. Tremendous."

Michigan led 14–9 at halftime and came out in the second half with a big defensive play. Allar fumbled when hit by Rayshaun Benny, and Makari Paige made the recovery during the opening drive of the second half. That gave Michigan the ball at the Penn State 49-yard line. Benny said Minter told them at halftime that one of the playmakers would make a difference-making play. Off that turnover, the Wolverines then went *smash*, burned the clock for just more than eight minutes, and ran 12 straight plays. The drive culminated with a 22-yard field goal by James Turner to give Michigan a 17–9 lead.

"The whole game our mindset was just having a pillar game," Johnson said as he referred to Minter's four pillars of defense they adhere to, "and strain the whole game, play hard, and do it for Coach Harbaugh. Our mindset was just play together, play as hard as we can execute, and execute the calls Coach Minter displayed for us. That's all we were thinking about. Get the ball back to the offense as much as we can."

The postgame locker room was, as expected, intensely joyous. In video captured by Sainristil, a large group of players began replicating the Penn State Beaver Stadium staple, the "Kernkraft 400" chant, which is usually followed by, "We are Penn State!" But, of course, they changed the words to, "We are Michigan!" Moore told his players, "from the bottom of my heart," how much he loved them. He emphasized the 32 straight run plays in the second half and that "defensively, you beat their asses." Moore announced there would be one game ball presented, and it would go to Harbaugh. The players then erupted in "The Victors," and Moore shouted to them the Harbaugh locker room question, "Who's got it better than us?" In unison they shouted their reply, "Nobody!"

Harbaugh met the team at the airport for the flight back to Ann Arbor. With the game ball under his arm, he hugged as many players as he could. Cornelius Johnson said the players were happy to see Harbaugh, whom he described as being in good spirits, but they noticed his voice seemed to be shot, more than likely, they surmised, from yelling at the TV. While being away from the sideline for the fourth time this season was not how Harbaugh had envisioned things, he took the opportunity to appreciate the Wolverines' resiliency.

"Just really proud," Harbaugh said. "I know I said it first team meeting, Moses had 90 leaders, how many do we need? Answer was we need more than 90. We've got that. We've got a team full of leaders. Future leaders that have already been galvanized. They were already on a mission. The mission last year was a happy mission. This year has been even more than the wins. It's a mission of faith, it's a mission of speaking truth to power, it's a mission of playing for each other as a band of brothers. It's a mission—I see our guys and they're strong, they're walking upright and innocent. Just taking care of business. The one-track mind. I'm so thankful for that. That's resonated so much. Wake up, take care of business, go to sleep, wake up the next day, take care of business again."

Wallace said at the NFL Combine that the Penn State weekend was significant in terms of the direction of the season. "Really, just the media turning it on us," Wallace said. "It gave us all motivation and wanted to play more for Coach Harbaugh. We were on the plane and found out that they had suspended our coach in the air. That kinda took us the wrong way. That's what kind of turned us around."

Upon arrival in Ann Arbor, the team, joined by Harbaugh, went straight to Yost Arena for the Michigan hockey game against Minnesota and were celebrated by the always animated Yost crowd. The players were shown on the scoreboard along with the word *Bet*. The football players were invigorated by the fans and waved their arms upward encouraging the cheers. A beaming Jenkins put his arm around Barrett, and they soaked in the enthusiasm, while fullback Max Bredeson captured the scene on his cellphone, and Sainristil, with his ever-present professional camera, shot video. Harbaugh, standing next to Corum, feigned placing a crown on his running back's head, the crown move a McCarthy signature. And then the chant began, "Free Jim Harbaugh!" The players joined in, as did Moore. The band played "The Victors" with the fans turned toward the Wolverines, and it culminated with a "Go Blue!" from the players. The music then shifted to the Penn State staple, the "Kernkraft 400" chant. The players began bouncing and embraced the music coming off that important win. Harbaugh then, with his left hand, gripped Moore's right wrist and raised his arm high, and they pointed to each other with their index fingers and grinned.

In adversity, they had found a way to celebrate.

– 10 –

No. 1,000

ALTHOUGH Jim Harbaugh was unable to be on the sideline with his team at Penn State, the Wolverines were feeling very good about themselves after leaving Happy Valley, and they set their sights on playing at Maryland, the final game before archrival Ohio State. They were emboldened—and so it seemed was Harbaugh—by the support from Michigan fans and former players, all of whom seemed to embrace the Michigan vs. Everybody mindset and also joined in on the "Bet" comment.

"Our team is already galvanized. They're already connected. They're together," Harbaugh said at the Monday news conference ahead of the game at Maryland. "Boy, I'm feeling a galvanized Michigan. A university alumni network and all the alums, largest living alumni body in the world for any school, and the fan base, which goes coast to coast and, and worldwide, really being galvanized. And that's a tremendous thing. That's a monumental thing when you think about it, everybody fighting like the team we're supposed to be, and that's gonna be tough to beat."

There was something about that Penn State victory that struck a certain chord with Harbaugh. He certainly loved the 32 straight second-half runs, and he respected the resiliency of a team that found out shortly before kickoff they'd be without their head coach to perform the way they did. He puffed his chest because he believed he had selected the right guy in Moore to lead the team in his stead. On the Monday following that victory, Harbaugh described games as his own children—you love them all, but some make you prouder. The victory over the Nittany Lions launched into his top five games. Then, in the face of NCAA allegations and rivals accusing Michigan of cheating, he made an attention-grabbing proclamation about the Wolverines.

"The perseverance and the stalwartness of these guys, I would have to say it's gotta be America's team. Gotta be America's team," Harbaugh said. "America loves a team that beats the odds, beats the adversity, overcomes what the naysayers and critics, so-called experts think. That's my favorite kind of team. Watching it from that view of the television, finally people get to see what I see every day with these players and these coaches."

Critics of Michigan's program mocked Harbaugh for referring to the Wolverines as "America's team" in the midst of an alleged sign-stealing scandal. ESPN's Paul Finebaum, who had long been one of Harbaugh's harshest critics, trolled him during an interview.

"What they're also not is Ohio State," Finebaum said on *The Matt Barrie Show*. "Ohio State is a much better program overall. It has tremendous tradition. I mean, if you're walking down the streets of New York and you get in a conversation, on most days, Ohio State is part of the front row of college football. Michigan's not. It's just not that big of a deal, and they take themselves so seriously up there."

Not that Harbaugh paid much attention to Finebaum. Maybe he did early on during his coaching career at Michigan when the two exchanged barbs, but Harbaugh was insulated from hearing the negativity. And seemingly empowered by coaching what he dubbed "America's team," Harbaugh made clear he was looking forward to the next step in the legal battle to challenge the NCAA. He seemed genuinely excited about Friday, when he hoped he could win a preliminary injunction during a hearing in Washtenaw County Courthouse in Ann Arbor to negate the Big Ten's suspension and allow him to return to the sideline for the final two regular-season games. He planned to attend the hearing and initially said he'd speak in court.

"I'm just looking for that opportunity—due process," Harbaugh said. "Not looking for special treatment, not looking for a popularity contest, just looking for the merit of what the case is. [As a] senior in high school, I had a civics class that talked about government and justice, and what I took away from that class was that you're innocent until proven guilty. That was 40 years ago, but I'd like that opportunity."

Later during the news conference, however, he said he wasn't certain if he would get an opportunity to speak at the hearing. "I'm gonna be able to go, though," Harbaugh said. "That's not my dance floor. I'm not an attorney. Always wanted to be. Watched a lot of shows. Watched Judge Judy a lot. Always kind of felt like it'd be cool to get up there and thunder away at a jury like Tom Cruise in *A Few Good Men* or be a judge, a Judge Judy, but alas, I did not go to law school. First time I've ever really been in this situation."

This was on the heels of the NCAA having investigators on campus beginning Monday to interview various individuals, including players, who may have been connected with or had information about Stalions and the alleged sign-stealing scheme.

There was a lot of anticipation that week, not only because of Harbaugh potentially speaking at the hearing, but the program was sitting at No. 999 in all-time wins. There is what's called the "Win Wall" in Schembechler Hall's Towsley Museum. It's a two-story, glass-encased, curved wall with rows and rows of footballs representing each win by the Wolverines. Each ball, which appears to be suspended within the case, features in gold the number of the win above the score, opponent, date, and location. Michigan, which played its first games in 1879, is the winningest program in college football and was about to reach a new milestone in the game: 1,000 wins. Quinten Johnson, a graduate student and defensive back, had given his family a tour of the facilities earlier in the season, and as they looked at the Win Wall, he noticed it running out of space.

"It's astonishing to see," Johnson said. "It's definitely a testament to the program and to how much history and lineage there is before you. You're definitely playing for something bigger than yourself. On the wall back there, we have a win count, and it didn't seem like that day will come, but the day's come. It's something I know I'm gonna take pride in 40, 50 years down the road just being a Wolverine."

The Wolverines at this point had won 26 straight regular season games and 10 straight road games as they headed into their preparations to play at Maryland. Harbaugh hoped to coach the team to its 1,000th win, and while there were no guarantees he would win the preliminary injunction, he was focused on getting the team ready for the Terps and also on ways to commemorate win No. 1,000. He suggested that maybe the "Michigan" in the Michigan Stadium end zones could be spelled with a "1G" instead of "1G." Of course, he said, M is the Roman numeral for 1,000. Harbaugh definitely had plans for a special sticker for the players' helmets to honor the achievement, and maybe there would be special suits for the occasion, as well as T-shirts and other types of memorabilia. Harbaugh is, at his core, fiercely competitive—whether as a player or a coach, on the field or off. Reaching 1,000 first fed that competitiveness.

"It's in our wildest dreams, that's what we hope for, that's what we worked for was that we'd have a chance to play in our 11th game this season. Chance to get that at 1,000," Harbaugh said. "And just really want to shout out the Green Bay Packers, most wins in NFL history, 793. Most wins in high school football, Valdosta, Georgia, 951. And Michigan Wolverines, 999. No one has won more. Nobody. And I want to thank, especially, everyone who has put on the winged helmet, [and] all those that have contributed and those that have supported their efforts. It's monumental and motivates us to find extra work to do, keep a one-track mind and get keener, finer, and more alert, get the job done. Very proud of our football team."

Harbaugh had started bringing up the one-track-mind mantra more and more. It always felt meaningful to the players, the whole concept of being where your feet are, as Corum would say, and that was tied into have a one-track mind. That applied to this week perhaps more than most. The Wolverines were 10–0 and were about to play the game before the Ohio State game. Michigan and Ohio State players think about each other all season. They practice each week preparing for The Game, while they ready for whichever opponent is that weekend. But when it's this close, the week before The Game, one game separating them from one of the greatest rivalries in sports, the T-word gets tossed around: "trap" game. Both teams were facing it. Ohio State was readying to host Minnesota, while Michigan was heading on the road to face the most talented quarterback the Wolverines had seen all season.

Maryland's quarterback, Taulia Tagovailoa, was leading the Big Ten in passing yards (2,769 yards), total offense (283.3), and passing touchdowns (22). He had a strong arm, and he was mobile. Should the coaches be concerned about the Wolverines looking too far ahead? "Not with this group we're coaching right now," Michigan defensive-line coach Mike Elston said. "These guys want to be good, they want to win, and you can't go to 12–0 until you go to 11–0. They don't want egg on their face, and they work their tails off every day to be in this position. I don't see this as being a trap game, I don't think our guys see it that way. I don't think that word fits in this program, and I don't think guys think of it that way. There's a ton of maturity."

Quinten Johnson was asked if he believed in the idea of the trap game. He responded philosophically. "I believe in the concept of a trap game if you allow it to be a trap game," Johnson said. "At the end of the day, the way I look at it, I don't look at Ohio State, I don't look at the championship, I don't look at the playoffs. I look at who we got Saturday, and it's Maryland. I feel like if you're always chasing perfection within yourself, or being the best version of yourself, the trap games don't really matter because you're not worried about the future. You've got to live in the present."

One-track mind. Be where your feet are.

"It's not hard at all because every single game since the beginning of the season, all we've been worried about is the next day," running back Donovan Edwards said. "When today's practice is over, we're going to worry about tomorrow's practice. And then Thursday and Friday, and come Saturday, we're going to vibe off how we practice throughout the week. And when Ohio State comes, Ohio State comes. We're just going to keep preparing for each game the same way we did in Week 1."

While the team prepared, business as usual, that was not the case for Harbaugh, who still planned to challenge the Big Ten in court, hoping to obtain a preliminary injunction to block the suspension that stemmed from the ongoing NCAA investigation into an alleged sign-stealing scheme. But on Thursday morning, a day before lawyers representing Michigan and Harbaugh, as well as the Big Ten, were to appear at a hearing before Judge Timothy Connors in Washtenaw 22nd Circuit Court, there was an abrupt change of course. Michigan and Harbaugh dismissed their lawsuit, meaning Harbaugh would miss coaching the final two regular-season games. Michigan issued a statement in mid-afternoon:

> This morning, the University, Coach Harbaugh, and the Big Ten resolved their pending litigation. The Conference agreed to close its investigation, and the University and

Coach Harbaugh agreed to accept the three-game suspension. Coach Harbaugh, with the University's support,
decided to accept this sanction to return the focus to our
student-athletes and their performance on the field. The
Conference has confirmed that it is not aware of any information suggesting Coach Harbaugh's involvement in the
allegations. The University continues to cooperate fully
with the NCAA's investigation.

University of Michigan lawyers pushed for this resolution with
the Big Ten, according to a sourced report in the *Detroit News*. However, it was indicated Harbaugh and his lawyers were not party to the
agreement. The agreement made with the Big Ten two days before
the game at Maryland ensured the conference would only consider
imposing any additional penalties if the NCAA concluded at the end
of its investigation that a member of the Michigan football coaching staff was aware of Stalions' activities and tried to conceal them or
were directly involved in helping him.

Moore would remain as acting head coach for the final two regular-season games. A day before Michigan and the Big Ten reached
the agreement, he was asked about the possibility of Harbaugh not
being on the field for the potential 1,000[th] win. Moore said if that were
the case, Michigan would still operate at the highest level possible.

The drama with wasn't over, though. There would be even more
fallout relating to the alleged sign-stealing scheme. At about noon
on Friday, the day Harbaugh was supposed to be in court hoping to
secure a preliminary injunction against the Big Ten, and just hours
before the team departed for Maryland, Michigan announced that
linebackers coach Chris Partridge was fired. Partridge, who had spent
five years on Harbaugh's staff before leaving for Ole Miss, where he
coached three seasons, had returned to work with the Wolverines'
linebackers in February.

"Effective today, Chris Partridge has been relieved of his duties as a member of the Michigan Football staff," Manuel wrote in a statement. He added that Rick Minter, the former college football head coach and father of Michigan's defensive coordinator, Jesse Minter, would fill in as linebackers coach. It was Harbaugh's idea to move Minter, a defensive analyst on staff, into that role.

The University of Michigan also issued a statement regarding the Partridge firing:

> From the outset, our focus has been on seeking due process and allowing the NCAA to conduct a fair and deliberate investigation. Although the Big Ten has closed its investigation, we are continuing to cooperate with the NCAA as it moves forward with its ongoing investigation. Consistent with our commitment to integrity, we will continue to take the appropriate actions, including disciplinary measures, based on information we obtain. Earlier today, Michigan Athletics relieved Chris Partridge of his duties as a member of the Michigan Football staff. Due to employee privacy laws, we are unable to comment further.

A story by Yahoo Sports said Partridge destroyed evidence on a computer—an allegation he would later dispute—after the scandal broke, according to sources, and while Partridge may not have known about the advanced scouting by Stalions, he tried to cover up evidence. A story in the *Detroit News* late Friday night said Partridge, according to two sources, pressured players to not cooperate and to be untruthful with NCAA investigators who had been conducting interviews on campus since Monday. The two sources connected to the university described the pressure Partridge applied to players, and that information was then disclosed to NCAA investigators, who then relayed the information to the Big Ten. This information made Michigan officials uncomfortable with proceeding with the preliminary injunction hearing. Just like that, the Wolverines were without its head coach on the sideline and now, permanently, without Partridge.

Partridge's termination letter from Michigan was publicly released through an open-records request by multiple news outlets in mid-December. In the letter written by Michigan athletics chief of staff Doug Gnodtke, there was no mention of Partridge destroying evidence.

"As we discussed today, the University has received evidence that you have failed to abide by the University directive not to discuss an ongoing NCAA investigation with anyone associated with the Michigan Football Program or others and as a result has determined that you have failed to satisfactorily perform your duties," the letter read. "As a result, your employment as a Michigan Football Coach is hereby terminated effective immediately and you will not be eligible for rehire at the University of Michigan."

There was no response from Partridge until two days after the end of the regular season when he revealed his stance in a post on the social media platform X. Partridge wrote that he waited to issue a statement until November 27 out of respect for the team and didn't want to create a distraction for the players as they pursued their goal of an undefeated season. Partridge posted this statement:

Unfortunately, the manner in which the termination of my employment and my role as a Coach at Michigan has been reported is inaccurate and has resulted in people speculating and making assumptions about my knowledge of, and connection to, the sign-stealing allegations within the football program. I want to be clear: I had no knowledge whatsoever of any in-person or illegal scouting, or illegal sign stealing. Additionally, at no point did I destroy any evidence in relation to an ongoing investigation. As explained to me by Michigan athletics director Warde Manuel in person on the morning of November 17, 2023, and as set forth in my termination letter of the same date, signed by Doug Gnodtke, Michigan Athletics Chief of Staff, I was terminated because of a failure to "abide by the University directive not to discuss an ongoing NCAA investigation with anyone associated with the Michigan Football Program." I take pride in being a trusted mentor to the athletes that I coach. One of my core values is to be a source of support, through thick and thin, for each and every student-athlete that I am responsible for. I have never wavered from that responsibility. While I am extremely disappointed by the University's decision to terminate my employment, their decision does not change my continued love and support of Coach Jim Harbaugh, the coaches and the players of Team 144 as they continue on their quest for a National Championship.

Despite all of that off-field drama, the players still managed to remain undaunted. They headed to College Park, some wearing MICHIGAN VS. EVERYBODY shirts, others wearing the latest addition to their apparel collection, BET T-shirts freshly printed coming out of the Penn State weekend. The Michigan football social media platforms posted photos of the players at the airport with the message, "On a Mission." One included a video montage that led with Herbert shouting at the players surrounding him, "We are on a mission, and they are standing in our way!" then Minter telling the players to "prove to the people that believe in us, that are here for us, that want us to do it, prove them right," and finally Jay Harbaugh saying to the players, "We all know where this train is going. Let's go full speed ahead." The themes among the team were clear, this was all about the mission, it was about seizing the moment and setting the tone, players said, and it was all about them, as they insulated themselves more and more from the outside noise that, while galvanizing, could be overwhelming if they allowed it.

The morning of the game, with a small group of fans gathered at the team hotel, an on-campus Marriott, the players and coaches quietly boarded the buses. Wilson wore a FREE HARBAUGH shirt that featured a photo of Harbaugh's face. They all were focused on what was ahead of them the next few hours. Everyone emerged except Harbaugh, who was at the hotel to be with the team through its departure for the game. Instead, he would get picked up to watch the game on television at the home of his older brother, John, the head coach of the Baltimore Ravens. Earlier in the week, John, at a Ravens news conference, spoke in support of his brother.

"His phones, his computers and all that stuff have been looked at, and he's come through this thing with flying colors," John Harbaugh told Ravens' reporters. "I don't know what they are trying to get, but they don't have anything of substance, and I just think I'm proud of him. I think it's a real compliment to our family and to him, something for us to be proud of. You get in this kind of a situation where you come under fire for whatever reasons, and you come out in a really good place doing the right thing all the time, and I'm really proud of that. He's a great man, he's a great coach. His players love him. His coaches love him, and he stands tall through all this."

Although coaches and players dismissed the whole trap-game concept, at least early on against the Terps, it felt like the Wolverines were distracted. Maybe it was not having Harbaugh on the sideline again, and maybe there was some shock to losing Partridge 24 hours earlier. There also were injury issues. Starting left tackle LaDarius Henderson did not make the trip because of an injury, Wilson, the team's leading receiver left the game late in the first quarter after taking a hit to the head at the end of a 23-yard pass play. Barrett sprained his left shoulder late in the first half but managed to return in the second half. And Myles Hinton, who started at left tackle for Henderson, injured a knee at the end of the third quarter, was helped off the field, and went straight to the locker room. Barnhart shifted from right tackle to left tackle, and Jones came in at right tackle.

Maryland wasn't making it easy on Michigan as it worked toward getting win No. 1,000. The Terps trailed 23–3 with 7:59 left in the first half, had a late score before halftime, and two touchdowns in the third quarter, which was notable because until Game 11, the Wolverines had not allowed a third-quarter point all season. A sequence late in the game allowed the Wolverines to hang on and remain unbeaten. Tommy Doman's 47-yard punt was downed by special teams captain Caden Kolesar at the Maryland 1-yard line for the Terps' final possession. On their second play, Tagovailoa was called in the end zone for intentional grounding, a safety that gave Michigan two points and a 31–24 lead.

With 3:36 left in the game, Michigan's final possession began at the Maryland 47-yard line. Three straight runs by Corum accounted for nine yards, and the Wolverines faced fourth-and-1 with 1:58 remaining. Maryland called timeout. Corum would make the yard and first down to essentially seal the game and the program's 1,000 victory. Michigan was 3-for-3 on fourth-down attempts against Maryland. It was a strong defensive performance again for Michigan, as Sainristil had two interceptions, Tagovailoa was sacked five times (including one apiece by Harrell, Barrett, Kenneth Grant, and Cam Goode), and the Terps were held to 15 yards rushing. Michigan also had two safeties—the first of which came off a blocked punt at the end of the first quarter.

"Maybe we needed this test a little bit," Corum said after the game in which he had two short-yardage rushing touchdowns that brought his season total to 20, tying Michigan's single-season record set by Hassan Haskins in 2021. "Maybe we needed a close game like this. Not saying Penn State wasn't close, but [Maryland] gave us more for our money out there. Guys like [Sainristil] had two picks and stepping up big, especially when the offense isn't doing as good as we wanted to today."

Michigan's offense wasn't as efficient as it would have liked this late in the season. McCarthy had a rare mistake before the end of the first half and was intercepted, his fourth of the season and first since Game 3 when he had the three picks against Bowling Green. It was his third straight game without a passing touchdown.

On the SECU Stadium field after the win, the team posed at midfield with football-shaped signs with "1,000" above a Block M. One group of players carried a rectangular sign that read, "1,000" while an adjacent group carried a sign with "WINS."

"This is gonna go down into the books forever," Corum said. "It just it feels great to be a part of, not only a university, but just a great team to go down in history with. It definitely feels great."

Moore would later joke that Harbaugh's photo would have to be edited into the group shot. Meanwhile, the Michigan fans, in abundance, began chanting "Beat Ohio!" as they looked toward the following Saturday's game against Ohio State for the Big Ten East Division title. In the locker room before Moore and the players went to the postgame interview room, they turned their focus to the Buckeyes. "And now, we all know what time it is!" Moore shouted to the players. "This is why you come to Michigan, is for this next game for everything in the Big House for a chance to go to the Big Ten title game. Everything you guys have worked for is for that moment next Saturday at noon."

Moore told reporters it was amazing to be part of the historic moment of winning the 1,000th game. "The guys are ecstatic to get that 1,000th win, but they all knew what time it was right after that," Moore said referring to Ohio State. "They all know what's ahead. Super excited for that challenge."

Barrett said he heard the "Beat Ohio" chants from the Michigan fans after the game. He also said that while the players have tuned out the criticism from rival fan bases and avoided the negative headlines, they have learned this is a team built to withstand anything.

"I tell the guys, 'Man, I've been through so much already, nothing can break me, nothing can pull my focus away from our ultimate goal,'" Barrett said. "We just got to keep that mindset. We all know what our goals are at the end of the year. We've been kind of preaching it from spring ball, since January. So just kind of going out, week by week, day by day, and just executing everything that got us at this point now. Just keeping that going through everything that's going on, kind of just airing that out and not letting anything really deter us from our goals."

For Barrett, Colson, and the rest of the linebackers, it was also a bittersweet win, their first without Partridge, a popular coach with whom the linebackers had bonded. LaTroy Lewis, a defensive graduate assistant who played linebacker for the University of Tennessee and briefly in the NFL, had been on staff at Michigan for two years and was charged with assisting Rick Minter in taking over this group.

"It's always bad to lose a guy like Coach Partridge," Barrett said. "He's great guy. Just having coaches to be able to step up, like Coach LaTroy did, he knows the scheme, knows the expectation, knows what we have to do. He's always been preaching it, he's always been around, always been just kind of that second coach throughout the year. It was never a second thought of can he do it, or can we be good? We all know what we have to do, we all we know what we're supposed to do, how we play, how we go about our business, and we just keep that focus the same."

Later in the season, Colson would share how difficult it was for him after Partridge's firing. "I built such a bond with him, so losing him halfway through the season was hard," Colson said. "But I know what he would want me to do, which is just keep playing ball, so that's what I've been doing. And Coach Minter, he's coached so long. He knows so much about football. He's a great guy to have in here, a great guy to learn from, so just always learning and always growing."

Christian Boivin, a reserve linebacker who blocked the punt against Maryland that led to Michigan's first safety, was asked the emotional state of the position group after Partridge's firing. "Obviously, a lot of emotion going into it, but we're ready," he said. "We're built for adversity. We have the depth and the coaching staff as well as the players to handle stuff like that. Obviously, the people who stepped up in a big way, coach Rick Minter, and then LaTroy Lewis, both of them stepped in, did a great job, and I think we settled in early."

Minter, the 69-year-old father of Michigan's defensive coordinator, was the head coach of the University of Cincinnati football team from 1994 to 2003. For Jesse Minter, it was an easy transition working with his father. Clearly, he trusted his father's insight and, having been around him in previous coaching stints, knew how he would handle various situations. Rick Minter had been a great help to his son all along, and Jesse called his elevation to linebackers coach a "great situation for us to try and keep the train moving as best as we could under those circumstances."

The players said they looked at the elder Minter as a "dad," a soothing fixture on staff at the most challenging of times. "He's like the Pops of the building," Boivin said. "Just a calming presence. With all that turbulence, he just came in, settled the room early, and then just made it clear that roles weren't going to change, the expectation was the same, and that we were going to prepare the same so we can play the same."

For Coach Moore, it was about continuing to steer the ship through the turbulence in Harbaugh's absence on game days. He guided Michigan to back-to-back road victories against Penn State and Maryland, but now it was on to the big one, The Game:

Michigan–Ohio State. In the moments after the win against the Terps, clearly he had turned his focus and that of the players in the locker room to the Buckeyes, but during his session with reporters, Moore said it hadn't hit him just yet that he would be the Wolverines' head coach against their rivals in the biggest game of the season so far. He joked that the only thing that had hit him was the fact his mother was coming to town for Thanksgiving, and he was getting prepared to be yelled at again for swearing during his post–Penn State television interview.

"I'm trying to take it a step at a time," Moore said. "We'll prepare our tails off for that game starting [Sunday] bright and early. Probably won't sleep a lot, which is kinda what we do anyway. It has not really hit me and it probably will as the week goes."

While the coaches began game prep early Sunday, after a morning weight-room session, Corum walked through the Huron Heights neighborhood in Ypsilanti, a city about eight miles east of Ann Arbor, carrying boxed turkeys stacked high. Each turkey was in an aluminum cooking tray and along he went door-to-door offering his Thanksgiving gift of turkey and a few gallons of milk. This was the third straight year Corum had used money from his name, image, likeness earnings to purchase turkeys to give to residents of underserved neighborhoods in Ypsilanti, where he had done community service. Corum, from Marshall, Virginia, has called the Michigan community his home away from home.

In 2021, after playing at Maryland, Corum had purchased turkeys and distributed 200 of them in two areas. The following year, less than 24 hours after suffering what would be a season-ending knee injury— he managed two plays against Ohio State a week after the injury but had to shut it down—he carefully navigated snow- and ice-covered pavement and delivered 300 turkeys. After the most recent win at Maryland, he was back again to help bring joy during the Thanksgiving week. This time, Corum purchased 600 turkeys and was spreading his generosity through three Ypsilanti neighborhoods that Sunday during Corum's third "Giving Back 2 Give Thanks" event, in partnership with Washtenaw My Brother's Keeper.

"This is a day I can count on every year," Corum said after making some deliveries. "It's going to warm my heart, put a smile on my face but also on a lot of others. I count on this day. I love this day. It means so much."

For Corum, it had always been about giving back. It was also his balance to academics and football and gave him purpose. It was his calm before the biggest, most emotional game of the year.

Michigan opened its 2023 schedule vs. East Carolina (a 30–3 win), without head coach Jim Harbaugh, who was suspended for the first three games of the season.

Offensive coordinator Sherrone Moore, one of three assistants who took over head-coaching duties during Harbaugh's first suspension, led the Wolverines to a 31–6 win over the Bowling Green Falcons on September 16, 2023.

Harbaugh returned to the sideline for the Big Ten opener after his suspension, a home game against Rutgers on September 23, which Michigan won 31–7.

Defensive tackle Kris Jenkins (94) celebrates Michigan's 52–10 road victory over Minnesota with the Little Brown Jug after the game on October 7.

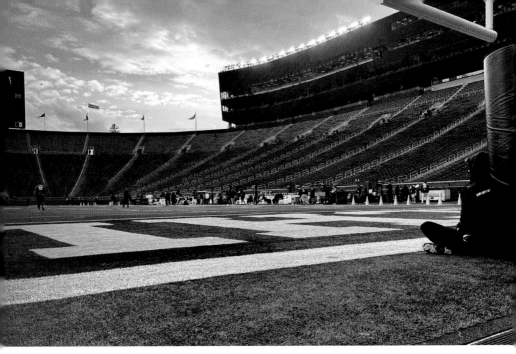

Quarterback J.J. McCarthy's pregame ritual included 15 minutes of solitary meditation. Hours before each game he would sit in the end zone, close his eyes, and find his balance.

Running back Blake Corum celebrates after Michigan's 24–15 win over Penn State on November 11. He had 145 yards on 26 carries with two touchdowns.

Right guard Zak Zinter lifts his fist in salute to the fans at Michigan Stadium while being carted off the field in the second half of Michigan's 30–24 win over rival Ohio State. Zinter suffered fractures to his left leg and would miss the rest of the season.

Sherrone Moore (above left) and Jim Harbaugh survey the field from the sideline during Michigan's 52–7 win over Indiana on October 14. Moore would once again take Harbaugh's place as acting head coach for wins against Penn State, Maryland, and Ohio State, before Harbaugh returned for the Big Ten championship game and the College Football Playoffs. Moore would become, with Harbaugh's endorsement, Michigan's full-time head coach after Harbaugh left Ann Arbor for the NFL to coach the Los Angeles Chargers after the end of the season.

Cornerback Mike Sainristil (left), surrounded by his Michigan teammates, holds up the Big Ten championship trophy after the Wolverines defeated the Iowa Hawkeyes 26–0 for their third consecutive conference title.

Blake Corum (above) evades an Alabama defender during the CFP semifinal on January 1, 2024, at the Rose Bowl in Pasadena, California.

Michigan linebacker Michael Barrett (above, 23) sacks Alabama QB Jalen Milroe during the Rose Bowl.

Linebacker Junior Colson (left) celebrates a stop during the Rose Bowl vs. Alabama. Colson wore casts on both hands for this and the Big Ten championship game vs. Iowa, and would keep the cast on his left hand vs. Washington.

Roman Wilson (1) catches a four-yard touchdown pass from McCarthy in the fourth quarter of the Rose Bowl to tie the game at 20–20 and force overtime.

Harbaugh flanked by McCarthy (9) and Corum (2) after they won the Rose Bowl CFP semifinal over the Alabama Crimson Tide.

Donovan Edwards (7), who struggled for much of the season, runs for a 41-yard touchdown in the first quarter of the CFP national championship game against the Washington Huskies, en route to a 34–13 victory and a perfect 15–0 season.

Harbaugh lifts the national championship trophy, while captains Blake Corum (2) and Mike Sainristil (0) and the rest of the team celebrate their first CFP championship and Michigan football's first national title since 1997.

– 11 –

THE GAME

AT LONG LAST, it was the week of The Game: Michigan vs. Ohio State. It marked the 119th meeting between the rivals—Ohio State undefeated (11–0) and ranked No. 2, and Michigan undefeated (11–0) and No. 3 entering the matchup at Michigan Stadium. This was the fourth time, and second straight year, both teams were undefeated and in the top three of the polls. A victory would launch the winner into the Big Ten championship game where the East Division representative would be penciled in as the champion, considering the West had not won in nine visits to the title game since the Big Ten was split into East and West Divisions. And a Big Ten championship would mean one of four spots in the College Football Playoff.

This also would be the last time the Michigan–Ohio State game would feel like this. With the Big Ten expanding to 18 teams because of the addition, beginning in 2024, of four schools from the decimated Pac-12 conference, the plan for the East-West divisional format was to go the way of the old Leaders and Legends divisions. In the newly expanded Big Ten, the top two teams in the conference rankings will play for the conference title.

In a division-less Big Ten, that leaves the possibility that Michigan and Ohio State could meet a week after their regular-season finale in the conference title game. Could that possibility dilute the season-ending rivalry game if both teams were poised to finished 1-2 regardless of the outcome? Maybe. The conference expansion added that possible wrinkle, but then there also was the planned CFP move from a four-team playoff to 12 teams starting in 2024, leaving another potential path for Michigan and Ohio State to meet yet again.

But this was the here and now, and while all those scenarios might play out in the future, both teams were only concerned about this year's edition of "The Game" on November 25 in Ann Arbor. Nothing could match the Michigan–Ohio State game from 2021 at Michigan Stadium in terms of ambience. With the snow falling, it felt like the game and the stadium were in a football snow globe— it was magical in that way. The Wolverines would go on to snap an eight-game losing streak to the Buckeyes, who had dominated the rivalry for two decades, and Michigan fans swarmed the field, releasing the emotion that had built up from losing so often. Again, this was not 2021, nor was it 2022, when McCarthy and Edwards helped lead Michigan to its first win since 2000 in Ohio Stadium. Still, even with that loss, Ohio State made the CFP semifinal. The stakes for this game were enormously high with the loser more than likely to be outside, looking in at the playoff.

Harbaugh would also be on the outside, looking in for this game. He would have to watch on television as had been the routine the previous two games he'd been suspended, as Sherrone Moore took over as acting head coach. Harbaugh still met with media for the weekly Monday news conference, though, and right off the bat he was asked about his level of respect for Ohio State coach Ryan Day and his staff. Harbaugh and Day did not have the friendliest history, but mostly in the sense of a war of words.

After the Wolverines' win over Ohio State in 2021, Harbaugh offered this statement without specifically saying who or what he meant: "Some people are born on third base and act like they've hit a triple, but they didn't." This was generally interpreted as a shot at Day, who had taken over the Buckeyes from Urban Meyer. This went even deeper, though. During the summer of 2020 and the COVID-19 pandemic, Harbaugh interrupted Day during a Big Ten coaches conference call and brought up a since-deleted photograph of an assistant coach on the field with a blocking sled and players, a violation of impermissible on-field instruction. Day, at a team meeting not long after that call, reportedly told his players that Michigan should hope for a mercy rule "because we are going to hang 100 on them." A COVID-19 breakout within the Michigan team forced a cancellation in 2020 of The Game in Columbus, so no one ever got to see the Buckeyes score 100.

Before the 2022 game, Harbaugh was asked if his third-base comment was meant as good-natured rivalry talk. He said it was "irrelevant, is what I think. I think that's irrelevant." The next day, on a Detroit sports-talk radio program, *The Stoney and Jansen Show*, Harbaugh referred to the comment as a "counterpunch" to the comment about hanging 100 and then proceeded to praise Day as a football coach.

So there was plenty of history between the two, and the question asked of Harbaugh about his level of respect for Day wasn't completely out of left field. It also wasn't surprising Harbaugh chose to deflect. "It's all about our preparation for Ohio," he replied. "The days, the minutes, the hours, everything leading up to this game, that's where our focus is, preparing ourselves and planning. We're going to practice then execute. Anything else is irrelevant when it comes to this big game week."

The next day in Columbus, Day was asked a similar question about his respect level for Harbaugh. He also chose to sidestep and move on. "We've just stayed away from all the distractions and focused on our team," he said.

Game on.

Michigan–Ohio State is always big no matter what the stakes. The old, overused cliché about throwing out the record books actually does apply to Michigan–Ohio State. And this year in Ann Arbor, the "championship or bust" approach was in full force among the Wolverines, because unlike 2022, when both teams managed to make the CFP semifinals, the window for the loser of the game to make it likely would be closed. This was going to be winner takes all, and that was the message Michigan players shared.

"If we don't win this game, the season doesn't matter," Keegan said, offering the most blunt statement by a Michigan player that week. "All of our goals are right there in front of us. We want to go to the national championship, we want to win the Big Ten championship, and we've got to beat the team down south in order to do that."

At this point of the season, there were layers of motivation for the Wolverines, way beyond the usual. It went from the TCU loss in the previous CFP semifinal appearance, pushing them in winter conditioning and spring football as fuel. But now they had other motivation, and their "Michigan vs. Everybody" apparel had taken on new meaning the past five weeks since the NCAA began investigating the program and sidelined their head coach for the final three regular-season games, including Ohio State.

"The thing we say, we don't care what anybody thinks about us," Keegan said. "We only care about the people in this building. Our opinions and what we think of this program is all that matters. We're really blocking out the noise. Obviously, there's been a lot the past month or so, and we get that, but we're doing everything in our power to complete our goals and do everything we wanted to do. It's right there in front of us. We know that, and we're doing everything we can."

Nothing said the Wolverines didn't care about what anyone was saying about them more than the "Michigan vs. Everybody" apparel. The sweatshirts had become a standard part of the daily attire for many of the players and pretty much illustrated exactly how the players were feeling. Corum showed up for Ohio State week media interviews in a MICHIGAN VS. EVERYBODY sweatshirt, which seemed fitting considering how much he spoke about missing Harbaugh on the sideline the previous two games and what his absence was doing to spark the team.

"Because Coach Harbaugh means so much to this program," Corum said. "He's formed a culture here, he's a player's coach, great guy we love. A lot of us would run through a wall for him. It's definitely been tough, and going into The Game without him, this is kind of just adding fuel to the fire. Not that we weren't gonna play hard at all, but we might play a little harder for him and make sure at the end of the game, we give a game ball to him. When you say you're gonna give a game ball to someone, you must win. We'll make sure we do that for Coach. It's been tough, but we know how to react to situations like this. This team is very strong-minded, so we're prepared. We'll be ready."

The players were also finding a way to make the "Michigan vs. Everybody" approach work for them. It infused them with a confidence and a swagger. All of the conflict they faced, beyond the opponent on the field, that's what they embraced. Seeing Michigan fans wearing the shirts made the players feel even more emboldened.

"I feel like it's a blessing in disguise because it's brought us closer as a unit, brought us closer as an organization, as an entire Michigan family," McCarthy said. "Just all the Michigan faithful reaching out and showing their support, it just means everything to us, and we are so greatly appreciative of it. It means a lot that we have all the Michigan alumni having our back, and it just gives us more motivation to get out here every single day and do our best for those guys but, most importantly, for ourselves."

Michigan's focus on Ohio State took a big step before the 2021 season when Harbaugh and the players altered their approach and began making the Ohio State game front and center. It always was The Game, but the Wolverines had not seemed to prioritize it like Ohio State had in recent years. At Big Ten media days in Indianapolis in 2021, Harbaugh spoke of the increased focused on the Wolverines' rival during Big Ten media days that July. Ohio State has long made it clear that the Buckeyes think about Michigan all the time during the season and Harbaugh intended to match that level of zeal. That off-season, Michigan added a "Beat Ohio" drill and more signage regarding the Wolverines' rival appeared in the football facility.

"We live by the motto, 'What are you gonna do today to beat Ohio State?'" Kris Jenkins said. "That's a motto we've lived by for two years coming up now. That's everything we started to work on, everything we started to build is for moments like this."

Michigan's starting right guard, Zak Zinter, said it was in 2020 during the dismal 2–4 season that the program changed the way it viewed the Ohio State rivalry. It was before the "Michigan vs. Everybody" apparel became a thing, but that's how he remembered feeling, and the aftermath of that season was the catalyst. "When it was the 2020 season, everybody was against us, and we wanted to prove something to everyone in 2021," he said. "We were both one-loss teams that year, and it was really gonna come down to whoever won that game was going to move on and keep going. We took that personal, and we wanted to prove to everyone outside this building we have what it took."

Zinter's offensive linemate Trevor Keegan grew up in Illinois, but he grew up in the Michigan–Ohio State rivalry. His mother is from Livonia, about a half hour from Ann Arbor, and much of his family is from Ohio. The Game had always meant everything and always had a different feel to him. It occupied a special place in his heart. Michigan had to win this game or the rest of the season would be a wash in his mind and that of his teammates. "This is a game we work for every day," Keegan said. "You see it all around the building—what are you doing today to beat Ohio State? Now that it's here, it's coming to fruition. All our work is gonna pay off, and it's going to show."

The night before the Ohio State game, Harbaugh and each of the position coaches spoke to the players. It was Harbaugh's words that most resonated with McCarthy. "The one thing that really stuck out at the end, the whole mantra, 'The team, the team, the team,'" McCarthy said. "He was saying we are that team. Everything we do from a character and from a hard-working and committed perspective, we are those guys, and we should believe it, embody it, and show the world."

Michigan would attempt to show the world with Moore at the helm again, who would later say he wasn't going to call the game "scared." He backed that up with aggressive play-calling, particularly on fourth down, adding a wrinkle with talented backup quarterback Alex Orji and a trick play, a halfback pass from Donovan Edwards to Colston Loveland.

It was Michigan's defense, though, that got the team energized when Will Johnson intercepted Kyle McCord deep at the Ohio State 25-yard line and returned it 18 yards to the 7. Johnson would later say how disappointed he was not to be able to get the pick-six. Instead, Corum, on fourth-and-goal from the 1, would score to give the Wolverines the early 7–0 lead. They'd build a 14–3 lead in the second quarter when McCarthy threaded the needle on a 22-yard pass to Wilson. Michigan took a 14–10 lead into halftime.

The Wolverines opened the second half with a long drive, including a 20-yard carry from Orji, who was inserted at quarterback for two plays. Turner made a 50-yard field goal to expand the lead to 17–10, but the Buckeyes found a rhythm. They drove 75 yards, including eight straight runs and a game-tying, three-yard touchdown run from TreVeyon Henderson.

So much changed for the Wolverines on the next drive. McCarthy connected on an 18-yard pass to Barner to reach the Ohio State 22-yard line when all attention turned to Zinter, down on the field in agonizing pain.

"When it happened, I looked back and Zak was screaming and Karsen was literally holding [Zinter's] foot, as it was just limp," McCarthy said. "It was a sight I don't wish upon anyone to see. And at that moment, seeing the look in everybody's eyes, seeing them rally together, there was something about it. It was spiritual, honestly. It was a different drive that came out of everybody after that happened because we're doing for one of our leaders and one of the brothers we all love."

The Fox television broadcast opted not to show a replay of the injury but panned to the concerned faces of right tackle Karsen Barnhart and edge rusher Braiden McGregor and Jenkins. The stadium of 110,615 grew silent, and a motorized cart made its way onto the field. Before Zinter was placed on the board to elevate him to the cart, his parents reached their son, and the entire Michigan team made its way to surround Zinter. His best friend, Keegan, was anguished and hit the field with his helmet multiple times while crying. Keegan hugged Zinter's parents before breaking from them to lean in to talk to his friend. McCarthy, Sainristil, Edwards, and Corum were the next to offer encouragement to Zinter. Jenkins, a fellow captain, would be the last to shake Zinter's hand before he was placed on the cart.

When Zinter was on the cart that slowly moved toward the tunnel, the Michigan Stadium crowd began to chant, "Let's go, Zak!" He was overcome and lifted his left fist to the crowd, then his right. As he neared the mouth of the tunnel, the Ohio State bench to his left was clapping for him as he moved past, Zinter looked up again and raised his left fist and gave a thumbs up.

Two weeks later, Zinter spoke about the emotions he had in that moment and after watching that clip, but he also was able to joke about it. "The way I look at it, they would never have chanted my name if I didn't snap my leg," he said, smiling. "There's always some positive out of everything."

Moore had to make a quick decision and moved Barnhart from right tackle to right guard to fill in for Zinter, and Trente Jones came in at right tackle.

On the next play, Corum broke a tackle and ran left to the end zone for a 22-yard score with 1:55 left in the third quarter. With the TV camera in his face, Corum immediately held up six and then five fingers to honor Zinter's jersey No. 65. Keegan was the first player to greet him in the end zone to celebrate.

"Zak's my guy," Corum said. "He's another guy who came back for unfinished business. That's why we came back. Seeing him go down in the last game hurt. Very emotional seeing what he was going through down on the ground. But we came together. We came together and we knew we had to do it for him, and the very next play, *boom*, we went up. I know he's gonna come back stronger than ever. One of the best guards in the nation. It's tough losing a piece like that, but I believe in my guys. I believe the next man's ready to step up, and I'm praying for Zak."

Turner made a 38-yard field goal early in the fourth quarter to build a 10-point lead, but Ohio State scored with 8:05 left on a pass from McCord to Marvin Harrison Jr. Michigan faced third-and-6 at the Ohio State 21-yard line, but Corum gained two yards. Turner added a third field goal to give Michigan the 30–24 lead with 1:05 left.

"I wanted to get that first down so bad so we could take a knee and get into victory formation, the best formation in football," Corum said. "I knew when we kicked the field goal and the defense had to go back out there, I knew someone was going to make a play. You practice like you play, and we practice hard."

With one minute left, Ohio State, with no timeouts, started from its 19-yard line and reached the Michigan 37-yard line. On first down from the 37, facing pressure from Harrell, McCord attempted a pass to Harrison but was intercepted by Rod Moore with 25 seconds left. On the sideline, Michigan legend Charles Woodson, who in 1997 became the first primarily defensive player to win the Heisman Trophy, helping lead the Wolverines to the AP national title that season, was captured by television cameras as he jumped and danced his way toward the end zone, pumping up his arms in celebration after Moore's interception.

Before the final play of McCarthy taking a knee, Michigan radio play-by-play broadcaster Doug Karsch handed a headset and the final call to Jim Brandstatter, the former Wolverine offensive lineman and longtime Michigan radio announcer. Brandstatter stood in the box, Karsch to his left and current color analyst Jon Jansen to his right and flawlessly finished the game coverage. "Wolverine nation, ladies and gentlemen, Ohio State is vanquished!" Brandstatter boomed into the microphone. "The Wolverines will win this and go to Indianapolis for the Big Ten championship game to face the Iowa Hawkeyes!"

The stadium emptied quickly as fans ran onto the field and celebrated with the players as they relished a third straight victory over Ohio State, a program achievement last matched from 1995 to 1997. Corum, the bridge of his nose bandaged after the Penn State game but still bleeding, was surrounded by fans on the field when he was interviewed by Fox Sports.

"It means everything to me," Corum said animatedly. "We did it today This is what we came back for, games like this in the Big House when your backs are against the wall and people think you can't do it, and people are calling you all types of names. But we stand strong, and we stay together as one, and we came out victorious."

Defensive back Rod Moore grew up in Clayton, Ohio, about an hour's drive west of Columbus and was never recruited by the Buckeyes. He came to Michigan as part of the 2021 class and always had a bit of a chip on his shoulder about being snubbed by the Buckeyes. This was personal, always has been, and the interception was some type of vindication for him. "It was a dream come true making a game-winning play on one of the biggest games in college football history," Moore said at the postgame news conference. He was still wearing the team's Turnover Buffs, a two-year tradition that involves whoever gets a turnover wears the Cartier sunglasses, called Buffs, and poses for a photo on the sideline with his defensive teammates. "I was on the field looking like, I just called game. I did that. I can't really explain. Dream come true. Just being from Ohio, the whole game was personal. Every year, it's so personal to me. Before the defense went out there, I told myself, 'You're either going to make the play or somebody else is to seal the game.' I told the [defensive players] up front they've got to get to the quarterback for us. I believe Mason [Graham] and Jaylen did and made the play."

He had missed the first three games of the season with injury. This made up for those absences. "Being a threepeat and being from Ohio, it feels great, especially them guys not recruiting me coming out of high school," Moore said. "Being able to beat 'em and get the get-back on them feels so good."

For Ohio State and Day, this third-straight loss to its rival was tough to stomach. "I tried to keep what we talk about in the locker room to ourselves, but we're all disappointed," Day told reporters. "We know what this game means to so many people and so to come up short is certainly crushing, not only just because you invest your whole year in it, we know at Ohio State what this game means. And so there's a locker room in there, it's devastated. And it wasn't a lack of effort. But again, we didn't win the rushing yards, we didn't win the turnover battle. So you're not gonna win the game."

The Michigan offensive players said they were overjoyed heading into the game when Coach Moore told them he was going to call his most aggressive game. That included a play he had stored from 2018 and was on display against Ohio State in the fourth quarter when Edwards connected on a 34-yard pass to Loveland on first down on the opening play of the fourth quarter.

"[Moore said] he's emptying the tank, and that's what he did," said Corum, who had two rushing touchdowns. "When we get in those fourth-and-1s, Coach Moore always says, 'Smash.' Then you have AJ Barner over there screaming in his Triple H voice, 'It's time to play the game!' It gets me hyped up, like I've got to score." (Triple H is a professional wrestling reference to Paul "Triple H" Levesque.)

Corum also said after this game, referencing Kobe Bryant, "The job's not finished, man," and said the Wolverines would get right back to work to get ready to face West Division champion Iowa in Indianapolis for a chance at a third straight Big Ten championship. Corum knew all too well what it meant to not be available for this next step. A year earlier, he underwent surgery after the Ohio State game, in which he attempted two carries before having to shut it down, his left knee unstable. He had suffered what amounted to a season-ending injury the week before against Illinois in the Wolverines' final home game of the season. Now Zinter, the team's top offensive lineman, would be sidelined.

His mother, Tiffany Zinter, would later post to social media that her son had suffered breaks of the tibia and fibula, or as it's often referred to, a tibfib fracture. He had been rushed to the University of Michigan Hospital and underwent surgery. Harbaugh raced to the hospital and was there about a half hour after the conclusion of the game. Zinter, his left leg wrapped, posed in his hospital room with his parents, Paul and Tiffany, and Harbaugh for a photo he would later share on Instagram.

The injury happened while Zinter was engaged in a block and an Ohio State player was blocked into him. He described it as the "best worst-case scenario," because nothing happened to his knee or ankle. It was a clean break and doctors stabilized the tibia, the larger bone, with a rod. About two weeks later, he started rehab on a zero-gravity treadmill.

"It was hurtin' pretty bad," Zinter said. "When the guy fell on my leg, I heard the pop, and I felt it, and I saw it going sideways, and I was like, 'It's really messed up.' I was just lying there, taking deep breaths and the doctor came out and straightened it and you could feel the bones moving around. That was the worst part. And then all the bumps in the cart up the tunnel and the ambulance. It was pretty painful until I got in the ER, and they put an IV in me and gave me some pain meds."

Despite the pain, Zinter continually asked for score updates after arriving at the hospital. He would eventually see the clip of Corum scoring the 22-yard touchdown on the next play and flashing his jersey number with his hands. He admitted feeling deeply emotional when he saw that.

Keegan and Nugent knew the moment it happened that their teammate had suffered a season-ending injury. How the team responded was representative of everything the players had done all season as they remained unified and unflappable.

"It definitely galvanized the team, and the next play we scored, which was crazy," Nugent said. "It was destiny at that point, honestly. It was pretty wild for that whole situation to go down like that. Seeing his season come short definitely inspires everyone. If anyone wants to complain, you shouldn't after seeing that. It definitely gives everyone an excuse not to complain."

Nugent and Keegan were as close as anyone to Zinter when the injury happened.

"He's my best friend and seeing him go down, his shin was right here, and my face was right here," Keegan said as he described being about a foot away. "I can't get that sound out of my head. I remember sprinting downfield and thinking, 'Ah, don't be true,' and then I turned around and saw him down and my heart sank to my stomach. I'm not an emotional guy, but seeing a guy who you've worked your tail off with and see him even change the Michigan program, all the hard work he's done, Blake scoring on that next play, our team, not just our team, but the 111,000 people inside of Michigan Stadium, that was the loudest I've ever heard Michigan Stadium. It really felt like our fans rallied around the players and picked us up. We were down. He's our leader. I'm with him every single day the past four years, and seeing the fans pick us up—Blake scoring a touchdown right behind my butt—it was a really special moment."

Nugent recalled Keegan taking on his guy, and Nugent looked over and saw Zinter's leg. "We all heard it," Nugent said. "It was like a baseball bat cracking over someone's leg. I knew instantly what it was."

With Zinter out of the lineup for the rest of the season, it would be on Moore to determine the best starting five. He had spoken all season about having about 10 capable starters, and in the heat of the moment of the Ohio State game, he determined moving Karsen Barnhart to right guard and having Trente Jones take over at right tackle was the correct decision. Barnhart was considered the most versatile of Michigan's linemen and had made starts at every position other than center. He'd played left and right tackle, particularly the latter, where he had made most of his starts. Jones had seen plenty of snaps during the season in Michigan's heavy set, and his linemates had often remarked he was the quickest and among the most athletic of the group. Time would tell if this was the starting five Moore would stick with heading into the Big Ten championship game against Iowa and its impressive defensive front, but this was the combination that finished the Ohio State win and likely would stick going forward.

Going forward for Zinter, it was all about being a captain and teammate and offering encouragement, advice, and even some coaching. "I've got my head up," he said. "Just trying to do anything I can to help this team keep on this journey and win these next few games."

– 12 –

THE BIG TEN TROPHY

EVEN without Harbaugh on the sideline for the last three regular-season games, including The Game against Ohio State, the Wolverines, with Sherrone Moore leading the way as acting head coach, secured another Big Ten East Division title and a spot in their third straight Big Ten championship game. They were two-time defending champions, and while no one would actually say it, there was very little trepidation about West Division champion Iowa. The Hawkeyes were last nationally in offense but relied on their fierce defense and acclaimed punter Tory Taylor.

This game would mark Harbaugh's return to the sideline after sitting out the last three, but at his weekly news conference two days after the Ohio State victory, he said while he understood the attention regarding his absence, he preferred to use the time doling out praise to the players and staff, particularly Moore, who he crowned a "Michigan Legend."

"I trust him because he's about the most trustworthy guy I know," Harbaugh said of Moore. "Like a brother. He believes in the players. He's somebody that's played the game. Had to do a job. You have to be brave, and players trust him. I knew when we came into the situations that he was the guy to empower to make those calls when the chips were on the line, because I knew he would trust the guys."

He ran down a lengthy list of players and their contributions in the Ohio State victory and pointed out how Barnhart had shifted from right tackle to right guard to fill in for Zinter and Jones jumped in at right tackle, exemplifying the next-man-up mentality. He credited the players for sticking together and playing for each other and for being the kind of team they had become through the 12-game regular season despite all of the outside noise. "For us, when we look at that sign, 'THE TEAM, THE TEAM, THE TEAM,' I think of this '23 team as The Team," Harbaugh said.

Now it was about preparing for Iowa's defense coordinated by Phil Parker, who a few days after the upcoming Big Ten championship game would win the Broyles Award as the nation's top college football assistant. Now, it was about gearing up to win a third straight Big Ten title and a return visit to the College Football Playoff.

For Blake Corum, this was an emotional week. A year earlier at this time, he was preparing to have surgery on a torn ligament in his left knee, suffered in the final home game of the 2022 season. His season—and Heisman Trophy hopes—had ended. While his teammates played for a second straight Big Ten championship, Corum was in Los Angeles recovering from surgery. But this was among the reasons he returned for a final season, to play for another Big Ten title and keep hope alive for a national championship.

"I remember I had just got out of surgery," Corum said. "I was in California laid up in the hotel bed with my dad and just watching the game through a screen. I could do nothing but cheer and think about what I saw through the camera, through the TV. It was very emotional. I wanted to be there so bad. Everything happens for a reason, and look at me now, I'm getting ready, I'm getting prepared for Indy right now. It's gonna be a heck of a time come Saturday."

During the week of the Big Ten title game, Corum and McCarthy were honored with the biggest individual awards in the conference. For a second straight year, Corum was named the Big Ten Running Back of the Year, while McCarthy was named the Quarterback of the Year. Michigan and Iowa would each be without a key starter—Zinter, the consensus All-American for Michigan; and the Hawkeyes' dynamic defender and returner, Cooper DeJean, was out with a lower-leg injury. Zinter, only four days after surgery, was dropped off at the football building by his mother, Tiffany, so he could spend time with his teammates and continue to be part of the process.

"We just have to stick to our roots. I don't think we should have to change anything," Corum said. "I don't believe in that. I believe when something is working, you stick to it. Maybe you sharpen it up a little bit and change a couple things here and there, but I think we have to stick to our identity. We have to play Michigan football. Obviously, Iowa is a heck of a defense. They've always been a heck of a defense. Just be ourselves, man. Don't change anything at all. Just prepare a little more and come Saturday, hopefully, we show that."

While Iowa's offense was statistically at the bottom in the nation, Parker's defense ranked fourth nationally, giving up an average of just 12.2 points per game and allowing only two rushing touchdowns. Minter and Michigan's defensive players were feeling the challenge in terms of which team had the better defense. But he wasn't shy in sharing that he had studied the Iowa defense during the off-season, specifically how the Hawkeyes put themselves in positions for interceptions and what the players would do after making the pick. Minter respected how the players immediately blocked after an interception with the goal of scoring points. During Michigan's off-season, as part of the four pillars, they studied and incorporated that facet. Picking apart Iowa's defense was paying dividends for the Wolverines, who were entering the title game with four pick-sixes, including two at Minnesota.

As the Wolverines focused on Iowa, Corum said that for the players, it was all about living up to the goals and promises he had made earlier in the year. It also felt even more meaningful because of the pressure the team felt from the two ongoing investigations, especially the more recent one that had cost them their head coach for three games because of Petitti's decision on behalf of the Big Ten. The Wolverines had never felt more galvanized and energized. Michigan vs. Everybody? The players were wearing those sweatshirts all the time, and that's how they felt they were best represented.

"I promised all these things," Corum said. "I promised to beat Ohio State, I promised to go to the Big Ten championship, and this and that, and we're doing it," Corum said. "Winning a Big Ten championship would mean a lot because we've been through a lot. We've been called all types of names. People don't think we're good at football because of this and that and just so much going on. Coach gets suspended for three games, and linebackers coach gets fired. Just so many things getting thrown at you. But what do we do? We're standing tall. We stood tall and we came together even more, and I didn't think this team could come together more than we already were, because this is a tight-knit team. We handled it in a mature way. Winning this Big Ten championship would mean a lot. But I like speaking things into existence, so after we win the Big Ten championship, we still have a lot to prove. But I believe our team is great, and we're going against a great team in Iowa, and I'm super excited about it."

The feel of this Big Ten championship appearance was different than the Wolverines' first in 2021. At that point, the program had not won a conference title since 2004 and was coming off its first win against Ohio State that snapped an eight-game losing streak in the series. This seemed, at least among the fans, more ho-hum, a short hurdle to leap so the Wolverines could get back to the CFP semifinal. Perhaps the most intriguing aspect of this game, considering the Wolverines were a three-touchdown favorite, was all the chatter about what would happen after the game, after a Michigan win. It would have been difficult to find anyone who believed Iowa would come out on top, not with that offense against Michigan's defense, even if it was unclear whether Will Johnson would be available at cornerback. The buzz before and during the game had to do with the postgame podium celebration. Namely, what might happen if and when Petitti took to the stage to hand off the championship trophy to Harbaugh?

That answer had to wait. There was a game to play. Harbaugh used his pregame speech to tell his players they had an opportunity to make history as the first team to win three straight outright Big Ten championships. The players said in that locker room, they felt a vibrancy from Harbaugh in his return to the sideline.

It wasn't the most thrilling of games, and it certainly wasn't pretty from the perspective of Michigan's offense, but the Wolverines blanked Iowa 26–0 at Lucas Oil Stadium on December 2 for a third-straight title. Johnson was in uniform and went through light warmups but would end up sitting out the game, a smart call to rest his body. Against Iowa quarterback Deacon Hill and this offense, the Wolverines wouldn't need him. The defense was huge and forced three fumbles, including two by Sainristil, who also had one of the team's four sacks and was named the game's Most Valuable Player. Freshman receiver Semaj Morgan had a spectacular 87-yard punt return, his first punt return of the season. It gave Michigan a spark, leading to the Wolverines' first touchdown and a 10–0 lead.

"As the ball came off the punter's foot, I was watching it in the air and I seen the gunners coming," Morgan said. "I kept looking at the ball and peaking at the gunners, looking up at the ball and peaking at the gunners. [I thought], 'Should I fair catch or should I not? It is what it is, I'm about to catch it and go.'"

Turner had four field goals, and Corum, who had to miss the Big Ten title game a year earlier, had touchdown runs from two and six yards to bring his career rushing touchdown total to 55, tying the record set by Anthony Thomas (1997–2000). McCarthy was 22-of-30 for 147 yards, improved to 25–1 as Michigan's starting quarterback, but did not have a touchdown pass for the fourth time in the last five games.

"Just back to the drawing board," McCarthy said. "That was a great defense, and I can't wait to learn from a great defense. We'll get better from it and continue to tighten things down to make us the most dominant offense we can be."

As the confetti fell and the Michigan fans celebrated, it was time for the much-anticipated podium meeting between Harbaugh and Petitti. The two men had a quick, cordial handshake before the post-game trophy celebration, and Harbaugh then asked Petitti to hand the Big Ten trophy to Zinter.

"It was special," Zinter said. "I was a little tired from crutching around after the game. I hopped up there [on stage]. I was the first one up there, and he handed me the trophy, and I raised it up. It's a memory I will never forget. It was super special."

Even the players were curious how the postgame exchange between Harbaugh and Petitti would go. "We were waiting for that awkward moment," defensive tackle Kris Jenkins said. "For [Petitti] it was probably awkward, but for us it was a little validating."

Jaylen Harrell, who also had a sack, said the validation felt satisfying. "I know he didn't want to give us that trophy, but it feels good all the hard work we put in," he said. "They counted us out. They told us we shouldn't be where we're at. All we did was stick together as a team. We did this for Coach Harbaugh. We came together, blocked out all the noise all year long. We didn't have our coach for six games this year. We've got to keep coming together. That's when we're at our best."

Mike Sainristil, who spent the first three seasons at Michigan as a receiver, had a dominant performance, and his teammates would later call him the glue of this team and, as Harrell said, the "tone setter," a two-time captain who showed up every practice and every game to give everything he had. He was the first to announce in December 2022 his return for a fifth season.

"Guys like me and Blake [Corum], this is what we came back for, to have the success with this team," Sainristil said. "The brotherhood that this team has is one that I wouldn't give up for anything in the world, and this team is going down in history. The way we go about our goals is you put everything into the next goal, and there's work, there's more work to put in and more ways to get better."

In the postgame news conference, Sainristil spoke passionately about his team and hit on a theme he would share a few more times before the end of the postseason. "Coach is probably going to say it, [but] I'm going to say it first before he says it," he said. "The worm has turned around here. The narrative has changed. For some odd reason, people look at Michigan and they'll say we don't play whoever, we don't deserve to be wherever we are. But as we say, the only people, the only things that matter is what happens inside Schembechler Hall."

"You took the words out of my mouth," Harbaugh said, chiming in. "You look at this whole group, and J.J., Blake, Mikey, so many others, the worm has turned. These Michigan football players, when you look back at the history of Michigan football, wrote the book on getting the worm to turn. The worm is pretty slippery. That thing can start wiggling back and forth and turning back on you. The hook got put in the worm. They've written the book on how to do it. It wasn't that long ago we were saying, 'We're going to do this or we're going to die trying.' They just give everything they got. That's all we ask them is to give it their very best, but they give everything they have on a daily basis."

For the players, it was a return to normal having Harbaugh back on the sideline. The three games without him were challenging, but what wasn't challenged was their resolve. Harrell said they all knew they couldn't do anything about getting their coach back for game days, but they could control how they reacted to his absence.

"We had to stay together and keep that feeling of us against them, Michigan versus everybody," Harrell said. "We kept that chip on our shoulder and blocked out whatever anyone had to say and got the job done. When people were like, 'Oh, y'all don't deserve this, y'all aren't good. Okay, bet. That's why you see all the 'Bet.' We're going to show you all better than we can tell you. We did a great job of sticking together as a team. It just showed [against Iowa]."

They wanted this for Harbaugh.

"We were going to stop at nothing to get him back to this stage so he could get that Big Ten trophy handed to him," Jenkins said. Jenkins credited Herbert for always harping on facing and dealing with adversity, no matter what form it is. Herbert would prepare them with things like surprising them in the weight room while they were doing a plank for a minute and a half and getting water poured on them. His point was to put them in an uncomfortable space and have them figure out how to do deal with it and determine what are they going to do now to change this adversity. It seemed after the Big Ten championship, the players wanted to vent about the finger-pointing and the allegations and what they perceived as people questioning how good this team really was.

"It's everywhere," Jenkins said. "That's where the term 'Michigan versus Everybody' comes into play. We've gotten used to it. It's unfortunate because as players we're used to putting in all this work, so to have all this hard work we've put in be questioned is kind of painful. It is what it is. It's the adversity we have to face, and we've gotta prove everybody wrong. We proved that no matter the circumstances, no matter what we face, who we face, we're not gonna break. We're gonna bend, but we're not gonna break. We still got that brotherhood together where we've got each other's backs. It doesn't matter what's going on, or who's out there because we're going to play for each other, because we're a team, we're family."

The players expressed joy in terms of their accomplishment of winning a third straight Big Ten championship, and they looked at it as a narrative-changing moment, but it also really was about this game being a stepping stone to their ultimate goal. Before Michigan's win over Iowa, Alabama defeated Georgia, the two-time defending national champion and No. 1 team in the CFP rankings, 27–24 in the Southeastern Conference championship. The Wolverines, ranked No. 2 heading into the championship weekend, likely would be No. 1 when the seedings were revealed the following day.

On Sunday morning, the day after the Big Ten title game, the team, staff, and coaches gathered in a ballroom at the Westin Hotel for a breakfast buffet. Around the rooms were four large-screen television screens locked on ESPN, which would air the final CFP rankings, the semifinal playoff matchups, and the rest of the bowl matchups. There was no real edge-of-the-seat concern in terms of where Michigan would land. The No. 1 seeding was out there for them and after winning the Big Ten championship as the No. 2 team, it seemed like a no-brainer. Entering the championship weekend, Georgia was No. 1, Michigan No. 2, Washington was No. 3, and Florida State was No. 4. The next four were Oregon at No. 5, Ohio State (which had lost to Michigan) at No. 6, Texas No. 7 and Alabama No. 8. Analysts were torn on Florida State, the ACC champions whose starting quarterback, Jordan Travis, was out with injury. FSU was down to its third-string quarterback. Would that be what would convince the Selection Committee to keep the Seminoles out of the final four?

Michigan players ate breakfast and talked to their teammates, a din of utensils against plates and chatter. A few players walked around the room and did the Florida State Tomahawk Chop gesture. There was a general feeling among them and some of the coaches that the Seminoles would fill that No. 4 spot and be Michigan's opponent in the CFP semifinal. The reveal showed Michigan at No. 1, Washington at No. 2, and Texas at No. 3. But then ESPN milked the moment before revealing the No. 4 seed, instead unveiling Georgia, the two-time-defending national champion, as the No. 6 seed.

Finally, it was time to award the spot opposite Michigan. Alabama popped on the screen. There were some groans of shock and then a few claps. Harbaugh sat at a table, leaning back in his chair with Robby Emery, a pastor and the team's chaplain, who also happened to be the head coach's personal assistant, next to him gauging the response. Harbaugh picked up a glass, turned to his left and smiled and then sipped water. Sainristil, at a nearby table, got up and was beaming as he went to talk to a few teammates. Harbaugh would soon after appear live on ESPN and speak with show host Rece Davis. "Thanks to God, first," Harbaugh said. "He's had His hand on this team the entire year. It's been a spiritual journey for us. It's a galvanized team. Some may think it's galvanized by adversity. It's not. It's galvanized by choice. Choice of playing for each other."

Videos of the Michigan players' reaction to Alabama being announced as their opponent went viral. Alabama fans, from several accounts, saw it as fear from Michigan players. The Wolverines said that wasn't even close to reality. "The media kind of portrayed it badly, especially when you saw some of those guys' faces," Junior Colson said. "They looked shocked, certainly, but the media took it as [being] scared. We're not scared of them."

"I'm pretty sure everyone in the room was, like, not scared, but thinking it was going to be Florida State or something. It was Alabama," Harrell said. "I don't think there was any scaredness or stuff like that. It was just like, 'Oh, it's 'Bama, not Florida State' type of thing."

Jenkins was unfazed and said he wasn't surprised at all by Alabama leapfrogging to No. 4.

"Unfortunate circumstance for FSU," Jenkins said. "That does suck. Feel for them."

Outside of the room, players spoke to reporters about being No. 1, Alabama, and having the month to prepare for a semifinal game they planned to win. Natty or Bust. It was always, Natty or Bust. This wasn't 2021 or 2022.

"The first year, that was our first time there in ever, and we played a great Georgia defense," Corum said. "I feel like, man, we were just happy to win the Big Ten championship, and last year we lost to TCU. We didn't execute at the highest level, we didn't take care of the small things, and the better team won. This year, we have to be where our feet are and watch more film than ever and execute at the highest level."

They had been there, done that, and understood the process now and the path to a championship. That the Wolverines would be playing in the Rose Bowl—a venue so tightly linked to the program and whose history was not lost on the players—felt magical to them, almost scripted.

"This is the moment I was born for, it feels like," Corum said. "Being able to be the No. 1 team in the nation first of all, play in the Rose Bowl against a great Alabama team, SEC versus the Big Ten, does it get bigger than this? I don't know. I know we're going to prepare like no other, and come that time, we'll be ready. We're blessed. I'm so thankful."

The players knew Michigan's track record in the previous semifinals. They knew on that first offensive series against Georgia's outstanding defense in 2021 that they were overmatched. Corum walked toward the tunnel after that loss to the eventual national champions, looked up toward the Michigan fans, and told them, "I promise you, we'll be back." They did get back to the semifinal in 2022 and, perhaps, overconfidence had set in as favorites against TCU.

Poor play-call decisions and a couple of pick-sixes from McCarthy put them in a hole, and despite a fierce response in the second half, the Wolverines couldn't get it done.

"We've been here going on three years in a row," Harrell said. "The feeling is kind of different. It's, 'Okay, let's finish it.' It's not like like, 'Oh, my goodness.' It's, 'Let's get the job done.' Knowing the feeling of losing helps a lot, too. We've been here two years in a row, going on three, so we know what we've got to do and what the preparation and the focus have to look like all week and these coming weeks."

Alabama carries a certain cachet. And after missing out on the CFP the previous season, this would be the Tide's eighth playoff appearance, most of any team, in the nine years of the playoffs. Alabama headed into this matchup with Michigan having won six straight semifinal games and was 2–0 as the No. 4 seed, including the 2017 national championship. The Michigan veterans said they were enthralled to see the Tide as their opponent and used a familiar refrain that to be the best, you have to beat the best. Corum was not intimidated, and he made sure to let everyone know what his and his teammates' approach would be during the next month of preparation.

"We are the top dog," Corum said. "We're going to approach it like we're the No. 1 team and they're the No. 4 team, but they're a great team. We're not going in there saying, 'Oh, this is Alabama, a team that's won, won, won, won.' Now, we're that team. We've been winning and we deserve to be the No. 1 team, and that's how my mindset is. The committee chose us to be the No. 1 team, so I'm not going to act like we're not. But 'Bama is a great team, so I'm gonna treat it like a great team."

Because Alabama is Alabama, the team was not some great mystery to Michigan. Linebacker Michael Barrett knew plenty about the Tide's offense, how physical they were upfront and quarterback Jalen Milroe's versatility. With the focus on a national championship heading into the 2023 season, the Wolverines had added a "Beat

Georgia" drill, a gritty, trench-focused competition. Harbaugh took a line from his friend Ric Flair, the pro wrestler and Michigan fan, that, 'If you want to be the man, you've got to beat the man.' That was what Michigan emphasized—to be a national champion you had to beat the national champion, except this time, it wouldn't be Georgia, but SEC champ Alabama. The "Beat Georgia Drill" would be renamed the "Beat Alabama Drill," but nothing else changed. During the drill, the Wolverines lined up a running back and two or three tight ends, and what you got was the type of physical bully-ball that had come to define Michigan football.

"This time around, I feel like we're more prepared, more ready, and more comfortable," Barrett said. "We have a 'Beat Ohio,' 'Beat Georgia' deal [separate drills] that comes into play when we have those teams who really bring it up front. You're gonna have a dog-fight in the trenches, and to prepare us for a time like this, we put that period in practice to get us ready, get our minds right for when that time comes."

That time had come. Still, as Corum had reminded all season, using the words of the late Kobe Bryant during the 2009 NBA Finals, the "Job's not finished."

"From the beginning of the year, even the off-season, we took a different mindset," Corum said. "We know we've been to the College Football Playoff twice but couldn't finish. It came down to execution, it came down to taking care of the small things, and when you play in a big game like this, you must execute at the highest level, you must take care of those small things—you must protect the ball, protect the quarterback, make the right tackles, be in the right fits. I believe this team with the leaders that we have, we'll be ready with our preparation. I know the coaches will have us ready, and I know we're ready to take that next step. This is our third time here, so you would think we would have learned our lesson and learned from our mistakes and be ready to advance."

These veterans, the ones who returned for another season at Michigan for this opportunity, were seasoned now. They had learned that what it takes to achieve the big picture, to win it all, is taking care of the small details. That's what allowed the Wolverines to galvanize, Harbaugh said. Maybe he was right that the off-field controversy had little to do with how the players had grown closer, how they had galvanized. Maybe it was about collected experiences feeling like they were paying off in terms of approach and preparation. Maybe it was simply that with a leadership group so deep, the captains and players like McCarthy and his role as a leader, they had infused the team with a belief that this would be the year.

A third-straight Big Ten championship was great but also seemed, to them, a foregone conclusion. Now it was getting even more real. Sainristil said after beating Iowa that the Wolverines were a team on the cusp of making history and that the way they go about their goals as a unified group was to achieve one and then put everything into the next goal and then the next. That way, it's always about getting better together. McCarthy was talking about winning a third-straight conference championship and said that in his eyes, "Act like you've been there before." It was something he and his teammates had picked up from Harbaugh, who had always harped that scoring your first touchdown should feel like you've scored your hundredth. In other words, Michigan now had cachet. They been there before, and they were acting that way.

"You can feel it through the players, through the team, through the coaches, through the whole staff, we've really got that mentality now that we're on a mission," Jenkins said. "With that mission, we've gotta go on a journey, and that journey, we've gotta get everything done. We've gotta check off all the steps, check off all the marks, we've just gotta take it one step at a time."

One step at a time with a goal of two more wins.

– 13 –

SEMIFINAL:
THE ROSE BOWL

COMING off a third-straight Big Ten championship and learning their CFP semifinal opponent in the Rose Bowl, the Wolverines took a well-earned, much-needed week off from football. After 13 games, the players were eager to rest their bodies and, perhaps more importantly, their minds. Football is a brutal sport physically, but a season can take its toll mentally, as well, especially for the Wolverines who had been dealing with accusations of being cheaters because of the Stalions sign-stealing NCAA investigation and also the growing noise about Harbaugh and his potential jump to the NFL.

This was an important week for players like Johnson, the standout cornerback, who did not play in the Big Ten championship game although he was in uniform. Johnson was dealing with a lower-leg injury and said his "best ability is availability," so the decision was made for him to sit out the game to be fully healthy for Alabama's receivers and the Rose Bowl. Colson continued to lead the team in tackles despite wearing casts on both hands against Iowa. He had been wearing a cast on the left hand since early November that was protecting the broken fourth metacarpal, an injury that occurred in the first half against Purdue, and yet he still finished the game. At halftime, X-rays revealed a clean break, but Colson demanded the medical staff put a cast on it so he could play the second half. He certainly needed a week away from football to give his hand a chance to rest.

Harbaugh and his staff, meanwhile, were readying for the early-signing period later in the month when high school recruits sign their National Letter of Intent, some choosing to graduate early to enroll early at Michigan and be part of the team's postseason run. He also took the time during that break to ask McCarthy if he wanted to discuss his future, the possibility of returning to Michigan for a fourth season in 2024 or leaving for the NFL.

"I told him, 'I'm only focused on 'Bama, Coach,' and he loved it," McCarthy said. "He was fired up."

That was not for show, an endearing moment between coach and quarterback. McCarthy remembered what it felt like to lose to TCU in the semifinal the previous season, and all that was on his mind was Alabama and leading Michigan to victory. He was not thinking about his future. "Nah, not at all," he said. "I'm completely in the present moment, soaking in every single day, enjoying every single practice, every single meeting with my guys. Only God knows that question. We'll know by the end of the season."

What McCarthy and his teammates knew—and were enjoying—was that Harbaugh and the staff had decided to take a new approach to practices that month during the two weeks after their break and before leaving for Los Angeles on December 26. Maybe it was time to try something different, considering the Wolverines had lost their two previous semifinals, so Harbaugh tweaked not the practice schedule but how they practiced. The players would not practice in pads as much.

"So it's been a little bit of a toll off our body," McCarthy said.

He admitted he and his teammates felt some fatigue mentally and physically heading into the Fiesta Bowl against TCU. Finding the right balance is always a challenge. Even during the regular season, some coaches have said they don't like the idea of a bye week because it can throw a team off its rhythm, while most of the time coaches and players enjoy a late-season bye as a way to get refreshed. McCarthy stressed this wasn't just about their bodies but their minds. "The last couple years, I felt like we fell victim to paralysis by over-analysis and getting over-detailed with too many things and overthinking things," McCarthy said. "I feel like we took things kinda light, easing into things, and it's been kinda fresh every single day. I think that's going to be the biggest difference in terms of keeping it balanced [mentally and physically]. I feel like Coach Harbaugh kinda knew that because the last two years we didn't win, something had to change. He talked to other coaches around the country and tried to figure out the best thing possible for us."

Harrell said that, while the practice alteration was benefiting the team, he also wasn't ready to blame their losses the two previous semifinal games on the practice schedule. "But I feel like in [Harbaugh's] mind he was like, 'Hmm, maybe we've got to change something we were doing differently the past few years,'" Harrell said, adding that the players were feeling a difference in their bodies and their recovery from the season. "We're out there rolling. Our bodies are feeling good, our legs are feeling good. Been competing on the days we compete, and on the days we walk through, we're mentally locked in. It's been good."

The defensive players found a balance in preserving their legs as much as possible while not taking it completely easy. By no means did they intend to diminish their speed and stamina, but by not having full-out contact every practice, toning that down, their intention was not only to keep the players from getting hurt but also to preserve and promote their mental edge.

McCarthy, like Colson, Johnson, and the majority of his team-mates, had been dealing with an injury. His was an unspecified ankle/lower-leg issue late in the season. He said like all athletes, he kept saying he was fine during the regular season knowing that it was a bit worse than he was letting on. He made clear he was 100 percent healthy and feeling good by the time Michigan began practices for Alabama. In their minds, McCarthy said, they were looking at this matchup with Alabama as Week 1.

Michigan also was adjusting to life without Zinter playing at this normal right guard spot as he recovered from surgery to repair the broken bones in his left leg. The Wolverines had adjusted for the Big Ten title game, going with the same lineup that finished the Ohio State game after Zinter was injured, with Barnhart at right guard and Jones at right tackle. Henderson was at left tackle, Keegan at left guard, and Nugent in the middle. Barnhart was the key, "Mr. Versatile" on the offensive line as he started the first four games of the season at left tackle before moving to right tackle to replace Hinton when he was injured. Moore said they were trying different configurations in practice, but he was not going to share details. He had seen enough from the line all season with four different starting combinations, and Jones had been vital as the sixth starter able to move in and out of the lineup when needed.

There were plenty of moving parts as is always the case during a season. Players were getting healthy, coaches were tinkering with personnel and how to get the best from the Wolverines, but Corum said there was a different vibe within the team, something definitely new but also difficult to describe.

"I don't understand what it is, but you feel it," Corum said. "You feel everyone just buying in from watching film to the practices and the way we're just having fun, the way we're flying around, the execution, the precision that we're playing with right now. It's amazing. Our execution is still top-notch and still precise. Every detail matters. I would say that's a different approach, just mentally. I feel like more guys are buying into the film, given this much time ahead of the game. When we go in the game, making sure we know everything that they could do."

That first week back to practice—the week of December 11—also proved to be an intriguing one because of some off-field movements. Alabama coach Nick Saban hired George Helow, who had been Michigan's linebackers coach in 2021 and 2022 but parted ways with the program in February 2023 to make way for Partridge. Helow was a defensive intern at Alabama in 2012, so he had some history with the program, but on the surface, it appeared the Tide coaches might be looking for an advantage as it prepared to face Michigan's top-rated defense. Saban would later say he chose to hire Helow as a sort of special assistant to the head coach because he had been at Alabama and knew the system. Because the staff was off recruiting, Saban said it was imperative to have someone, in this case, Helow, getting a scouting report prepared to have ready upon the staff's return.

Barrett saw the news that his former position coach had been hired by Alabama and then shared it with Colson. Colson said he was happy Helow had a job and joked he might greet him with a "What's up?" after the game.

"Just different," Colson said, smiling. "It's like, huh, they might be a little scared. You never know."

Colson said he really didn't think Helow could help Alabama much in terms of offering secrets to picking apart the Michigan defense. "You can't really have an advantage in football," Colson said. "It doesn't matter if you know somebody's whole playbook, you've still got to stop it. You've just got to go out there and play ball and let the dice roll how they roll."

Another interesting development, which was not confirmed until later in the month but was known in Harbaugh's very tight circle of confidants, was that Harbaugh had hired high-powered Los Angeles–based agent Don Yee, mostly known for his NFL ties. He represents seven-time Super Bowl–champion and former Michigan quarterback Tom Brady, as well as Denver Broncos coach Sean Payton, among others. Harbaugh was never known to rely on agents, so this was a major move as he negotiated a long-term deal with Michigan—Yee had met with University of Michigan president Santa Ono earlier in December to discuss Harbaugh's contract—while also keeping his NFL options open.

Still, while there was hand-wringing among the Michigan fans, who absolutely wanted a mutual commitment between Harbaugh and the university, the bottom line was preparing for the Rose Bowl, getting the next two wins, and a national championship. Corum had never wavered in what he believed this team could achieve. Even seeing Michigan as slim 1.5-point favorites over Alabama and the aura of the Tide, which had won national championships in 2015, 2017, and 2020 after the CFP was created in 2014, he didn't blink.

"For me, it's natty or bust, and we're that close," said Corum, who walked off the field after losing the 2021 semifinal to eventual national champion Georgia saying Michigan would return in 2022. "We have to find a way to get over that hump, and I think we will. I think we have the recipe. Now it's just about being where our feet are these next couple of days, until we leave for Cali. And when we get to Cali, still being where our feet are until January 1, and making sure we're just precise. We can't make any mistakes."

It was clear to Corum even shortly after the four teams in the CFP were announced that Michigan as the top seed would be overshadowed by No. 4 Alabama. He believed Alabama was being looked at as the nation's No. 1 team, and in reality, Corum was fine with that because it was providing more fuel for the Wolverines, who had felt undervalued, underappreciated, and yes, disrespected most of the season.

"Yeah, they flipped from the jump. As soon as they announced we'd be playing Alabama, I feel like they flipped it," Corum said, referring to the national narrative of the matchup. "Which is fine. It's all people's opinions and what they think. We're going into it, like I said [after the selection show on December 3], as the top dog. We are the No. 1 team in the nation, and we're gonna treat it as such. Alabama is a great team. After watching film, they're coached really well. Defense flies around, so it's definitely gonna be a challenge that we're super excited for. We love a good challenge, but we're still the top dog, and that's how we're going in."

Minter knew that Milroe, Alabama's quarterback, would be the headline stealer of the Rose Bowl and that played into the Wolverines' confident but underdog approach. He cleverly referred to the CFP as the "Alabama Invitational" because the Tide had participated in eight of 10 playoffs under this format and juxtaposed that to Michigan's failure to win in its first two semifinal appearances. His players had described Minter not only as a brilliant strategist but masterful at motivating them. He built them up but he never let them rest, and the result was a constant desire to improve.

"The group has been driven to get to this moment," Minter said. "Past failures often lead to that mentality, the chip on your shoulder. Even though we've had the success and it's great, nobody is ever going to take that away. It's really this moment. To a man, everybody said this is what we're gunning for, this is why we're coming back. That's why all the wins along the way are so crucial because it kept you on path to get here. Now we're here, and now it's on us to try and get further than we have and reach our ultimate destination. It doesn't guarantee that, but our mentality of feeling hungry, [feeling] like we're the underdog [helps]. Let's go. Let's bring on the best, and let's play them and see where we're at."

As they made their final preparations in Ann Arbor, the Wolverines knew how much more they'd be exposed to national media once they arrived in Los Angeles. While the local beat writers had followed the NCAA investigations all along, this would be the first opportunity for most national reporters to have a chance to talk to players about the season of distractions and how being without Harbaugh for six regular-season games affected them. The Wolverines had also lost a coach late season in Partridge, heard the Harbaugh-to-the-NFL talk heating up, and dealt with plenty of rivals bringing up the possibility of the NCAA forcing Michigan to vacate wins.

It was a a lot, and all of it fed the chip-on-the-shoulder approach of the Wolverines.

"I've always felt like we're underdogs no matter what—No. 1, No. 2, No. 3, 4, 25—whatever we're ranked. I just feel like we're underdogs because of many different reasons," Sainristil said. "You know, our schedule wasn't the best, they say Coach Moore stepping in doing what he did, even then, that wasn't good enough. We don't care about that. We just care about the fact we want to prove that we are who we say we are, not about what anyone else thinks about us."

Sainristil then explained who the Wolverines really are and what defines them. "A team that loves each other, a team that cares about the program, a team that's willing to do anything for the guys in the program. And that's been displayed in multiple ways this year," he said. "And a team that, no matter what you say about us, it's not going to affect us because we only care about ourselves. We're not looking to prove anything to you that isn't a reflection of who we are."

While the Wolverines were busy practicing and readying for Alabama, the NCAA issued a Notice of Allegations to the Michigan athletics department on December 18 for the first investigation that involved, in part, impermissible recruiting visits during a COVID-19 recruiting dead period. Michigan only publicly acknowledged the receipt of the NOA and did not share its contents. Bottom line, it would have zero effect on the players as they worked toward their goal.

Michigan departed for Los Angeles the day after Christmas, and on December 27, the Rose Bowl activities commenced with both Michigan and Alabama visiting the Disneyland resort in Anaheim and participating in a parade down Main Street, accompanied by Mickey Mouse and Minnie and all the Disney characters. Harbaugh sat in the front of the first white carriage drawn by a white horse and waved to the crowd with his family right behind him. In the next carriage adorned with, what else, red roses, Jenkins, Corum, and Sainristil waved to the fans. Just behind were Alabama coach Nick Saban and his wife, followed by several of the 'Bama players.

It was the first opportunity for media to chat with Harbaugh and a few of the players before they headed off for the rides at Disney. Naturally, Harbaugh, who had turned 60 two days before Christmas, was asked about his future, especially since he was so close to one of the potential rumored NFL destinations, the Los Angeles Chargers. This was becoming a December-January rite the last few years. On the heels of Michigan's success in 2022, Harbaugh flew to Minneapolis that February and interviewed for the Vikings job. He did not receive an offer. In early 2023, not long after Michigan received the draft of the NCAA Notice of Allegations for the first investigation, he was in conversations with the Denver Broncos.

So here it was again, late December, and the NFL rumors were swirling as Michigan approached its third straight CFP semifinal. He was asked his response to the recent NFL speculation.

"Such a one-track mind. That's the way we're going about things," Harbaugh said, not surprisingly deflecting. "Literally, whatever day we're in, looking to get the most out of it, dominate the day, then we're going to sleep tonight and wake up tomorrow and see if we can't dominate that day. It's a single-minded group. Just very focused on taking care of business today and see if we can't do the same tomorrow."

He was then asked by a Los Angeles–based sportswriter about his history playing for the Chargers in 1999–2000. "Just a one-track mind about this game," Harbaugh said, sidestepping the question. "Right now, having fun with the family and the team and the players. We're at the happiest place on earth and we're gonna enjoy ourselves. Then get back to business."

In a season of distractions, this became another for the players to ignore. Without a doubt, they had learned to compartmentalize and focus on the only thing that mattered—playing football and winning.

"It's happened a couple times," Corum said of the Harbaugh NFL rumors. "We don't really pay attention to it. Maybe it's people just trying to distract you and put all this stuff in the media. It's happened all year, so we don't really pay attention to that."

The questions then turned to McCarthy and how much his body benefited from the break and the less-intense practices. Harbaugh said his quarterback was moving well, so was the entire team, and they had had a solid, brisk practice and looked "sharp" that day before heading to Disney. Before the start of the season, Harbaugh predicted to Fox Sports' Bruce Feldman that Michigan could have 20 players invited to the NFL Combine in Indianapolis in late February in advance of April's NFL Draft. One of those possible players was McCarthy, who had notably told Harbaugh weeks earlier he didn't want to take his attention from Alabama prep to discuss his future. "Oh yeah, I think he's NFL-ready," Harbaugh said while at Disneyland. "Like he said, he wanted to just wait and play the game. Single-track mind, one-track mind. Love it. Let's keep doing that because that's what got us here."

Harbaugh would not share the advice he planned to give McCarthy and again sidestepped the question by reiterating that the team's goal was to beat Alabama in the Rose Bowl. "It's exactly where we wanted to be," Harbaugh said. "Our guys deserve to be congratulated for putting themselves in this position, as does Alabama, two great programs facing off in a playoff atmosphere. It's as good as it gets at this stage. We're honored and excited to be here. The happiest place on earth is a winning locker room. So we could be at the happiest place on earth today, and we've got a chance to be in the happiest place on earth, which would be a winning locker room at the Rose Bowl."

Bowl games had been tough on Harbaugh-coached Michigan teams, which were 1–6 entering the Rose Bowl. The Wolverines' defense had its focus on Milroe. The 6'2", 220-pound redshirt sophomore had completed 171-of-261 passes for 2,718 yards, 23 touchdowns, and six interceptions, and was 'Bama's third-leading rusher with 468 yards on 140 carries and 12 touchdowns. Milroe ranked fifth in passing yards per completion (15.89).

There had been some growing pains early in the season for Milroe, who, after a 34–24 loss to Texas, sat the next game at UCF. In that loss to Texas, he threw for 255 yards, two touchdowns, two interceptions, and took five sacks. He'd regained the starting job when Alabama opened Southeastern Conference play. Minter was impressed. Michigan had not faced a quarterback with Milroe's talent all season, the closest being Maryland's Tagovailoa, whom the Wolverines saw during their final regular-season road game. Milroe could run, throw, and make off-schedule plays.

"He's talented, real athletic, freaky," Harrell said of Milroe. "As an edge guy, it's gonna be a big game with containing him in the pocket. I'm not trying to do too much, because if you get out of your lane, he can take it 100 yards. So just playing great cohesive defense to stop him and slow him down. It's all of us—the defensive line, all the backers, everyone, even some of the guys in coverage, keeping eyes back, because one guy gets out of his lane, could be a problem. It's going to be a lot of unselfish pass rush this game. We have got to have containment in the pocket and get coverage sacks and stuff like that."

Michigan turned to Orji, the sophomore backup quarterback comparable in size to Milroe at 6'3", 236 pounds, and similar, although not nearly as polished without the considerable game experience, in skill. Harbaugh had called him the "scariest, most athletic" player on the team. Orji would be assigned to run the scout-team offense and give the defense a look that would prepare those players for the Alabama quarterback. Orji tends to watch film of other quarterbacks, so studying Milroe was not exactly new to him. They're both from Texas, so Orji got a chance to see him in high school and said what made Milroe so tough to defend was his ability to create.

"It's never forced. It's real natural for him, just a naturally dynamic athlete, really explosive," Orji said. "Also, his willingness to sit in the pocket. I think a lot of the time people want to say he's just a runner, he just wants to tuck it and run, but you watch games, he really wants to drop back, and when the opportunities present themselves, he makes people pay. I'm just trying to make the scout team pay as much as possible. Sometimes I'll talk a little trash to [defensive tackles] KG [Kenneth Grant] and Mason [Graham] here and there, try to get their legs moving, and they've done a great job reacting to it."

Michigan entered the Rose Bowl leading the nation in scoring defense, allowing an average of 9.5 points per game; second in total defense (239.7 yards per game) and passing defense (152.6 yards); and fifth against the run (87.1 yards). This was about as complete a defense as it could be. Milroe would say during interviews before the game that Georgia's defense, which Alabama beat in the SEC title game to leapfrog into the four-team playoff, was "more complex" than Michigan's but was comparable in terms of physicality.

"I think Michigan has a better defense [that] has been playing together for a long time," Milroe said. "I think that's something that's allowed them to be successful, and it's how they play well together. There's a reason why they're undefeated."

Michigan's defenders praised Orji for his simulation of Milroe, who is quick and moves a lot, so they needed to be on their toes at all times. Jenkins said the Wolverines' pass rush would have to be at its best and could not let Milroe out of the pocket. Colson wondered aloud if Milroe, with his powerful arm, might throw more than most anticipated. With that in mind and knowing his ability to break out and run, Colson said the defense had to keep everything in front of it.

"You just can't let him tear down your defense," Colson said.

Harrell, as one of Michigan's top edge rushers, relished the opportunity to go against Milroe and spoke animatedly about the matchup. The best against the best, he said, a challenge he embraced. "He plays playground football, so we have gotta keep going 'til the whistle stops," Harrell said. "It's 11 hats flying around each and every play. You can't go into the game shy or thinking too much, but then if you slow down, he's back there all day. It's gotta be a nice balance. You gotta be aggressive, but you can't do too much and let him escape out the back door for 90 yards. We have to find that balance."

The days before the Rose Bowl were not without some controversy. Alabama players revealed during a media session that their coaches had suggested they no longer use their individual tablets for film study and used the Michigan sign-stealing allegations as the reason why. The players, now no longer allowed to watch the film on their own, had to go to a larger room in the team hotel designated for film watching. "We were able to watch film as a team, but personally we can't watch film because, I don't know, some reason Michigan stealing signs," Alabama receiver Isaiah Bond told reporters at a Rose Bowl media session. "Our coaches told us that probably like a week ago, right before we left to come here."

Michigan's offensive players and coaches had an interview session the next day, and Moore shared that back in November, the Wolverines also stopped having players use their tablets to watch film and said Michigan had "caught wind" of tampering from other teams. The players had been meeting as position groups before or after practice to review film. The concern revolved around software technology from Australian-based sports analytics company Catapult Sports. Catapult released a statement saying it had not found any sort of security breach in its systems but was aware of an "ongoing investigation of the alleged unauthorized access to NCAA football video footage."

The players shrugged off the implications and said the change to their routine in terms of being able to watch film off their own tablets had not affected them. Nugent said the Wolverines had shut down tablet use just before the Penn State game in early November, and there were no issues among players or coaches in terms of heading to the football building to study film.

"Guys are in the building probably as much as they are at home," Moore said. "Maybe even more sometimes. I don't think it impacts [much]. I think it impacts that they can't watch it at their houses and lay in their own beds sometimes. But maybe it might help, because the next thing they would do is play Call of Duty. So maybe it does help that way."

Two days before the Rose Bowl, the teams were scheduled to take team photos in the stadium before separate, massive media days where every player and coach was made available for interviews. Inclement weather forced the cancellation of those team photos, and Michigan decided to change its routine that day from practicing at Dignity Health Sports Park, home of the L.A. Galaxy of Major League Soccer, where both teams had practiced during the week, to SoFi Stadium where the Rams and Chargers play. The irony wasn't lost on those tied up in the Harbaugh-to-the-NFL rumors, especially considering the Chargers seemed to be a team that likely would be very much in play if he decided to flirt again with the NFL. Harbaugh's agent, Don Yee, who had attended a Michigan practice earlier in the week with his business partner, Steve Dubin, dropped by the Rose Bowl media day to visit with Harbaugh.

McCarthy, meanwhile, was definitely feeling confident. When asked during this trip whether he felt prepared to take the next step and play in the NFL, he offered an enthusiastic response and said he did feel good about where his game was at that point. He might have been influenced by hearing Harbaugh's comments about being NFL-ready, but McCarthy seemed different during this leadup to the CFP semifinal versus a year earlier before facing TCU.

"I feel like last year I got caught up in the noise and all the emotions of it," McCarthy said. "And I'm just trying to stay simple, trying to focus on dominating meetings, dominating practice, and just being around my guys and enjoying every moment because this only comes around once for us, and just appreciating every moment."

McCarthy said the team had adjusted well to Harbaugh's decision to alter the practices and praised his coach for taking advice from other coaches and even the players as he made the call to limit the amount of hitting in practices. McCarthy said their game preparations had been smooth, effortless, and they also were having fun, whether it was the annual Rose Bowl excursion to Lawry's for the "Beef Bowl," where players dined on prime rib and watched Keegan handle the salad spinning and Jenkins the meat slicing, or playing games set up at the tables under the giant white tent for media day. McCarthy decided to take his Rose Bowl experience a step further with customized cleats for the game, designed and painted by Jada Henderson, the wife of Wolverines left tackle LaDarius Henderson. She does intricate work on shoes for a number of professional athletes, and McCarthy requested something simple but special. She painted a stem with two roses on the back of each shoe.

Throughout the season, Harbaugh would have a number of different people, including former players, speak to the team, typically on Fridays. Michigan had not been to the Rose Bowl since January 2007, a 32–18 loss to USC, and three trips prior to that game was the program's last Rose Bowl victory, a 21–16 win over Washington State on January 1, 1998, which wrapped up an undefeated 1997 season and the AP national championship. Michigan played in the very first Rose Bowl in January 1902 and defeated Stanford 49–0. Its ties with the Rose Bowl are deep, and with the Michigan alumni base in Los Angeles numbering about 10,000 and fans eager to travel to Pasadena, the Wolverines were expecting an enormous turnout. To shed light on the importance of the Rose Bowl as a venue and as a game, Jansen, a two-time captain and offensive lineman on the 1997 team, who currently works as the team's radio analyst on game broadcasts, spoke to the team on December 27. Jansen had deep ties with this program, not only because of his role on the radio broadcast but because of his work hosting the weekly in-season Monday night radio show, as well as a number of in-house podcasts.

Jansen shared with the players why the Rose Bowl is called the "Granddaddy of Them All," a nickname from the late television broadcaster Keith Jackson, but he also used the time to share with them what it means to be a national champion. Sure, he knew they were playing the Rose Bowl and Alabama for a chance to play for the national title a week later, but this team had never been shy about its ultimate goal, so he took the opportunity to share with them how a national title will affect their lives, the camaraderie it develops that will last the rest of their lives.

"They want to be able to talk to guys from that '97 team, and they want to know what it's like, so they know what they're going for," Jansen said.

On New Year's Eve, the day before the game, Harbaugh and Saban met the media for one final pregame news conference. There were the usual platitudes and nothing earth-shattering in the questions and answers, until the end when things seemed to grow uncomfortable.

Saban fielded the last question of the news conference: "Nick, are you concerned with the sign-stealing stuff out of Michigan, and what has Alabama done to prevent some of that?" As Saban answered, with the two men separated by a display of red roses and the Rose Bowl trophy with the Alabama and Michigan helmets in front, Harbaugh shifted and seemed uncomfortable.

"No, we're really not concerned about that," Saban said. "Integrity in the game I think is really, really important, and our team has had every opportunity to prepare for this game just like they have every other game. I think that especially when you're a no-huddle team you've got to adapt and adjust how you communicate with the quarterback, and hopefully one day we'll get to the NFL system where you can just talk to the guy in his helmet. I think that would be a lot better. But for now, we just have to adapt to how we communicate with the quarterback, and we'll change it up and try to not put our players at a disadvantage in any way."

Harbaugh continued to look forward at the rows of reporters as Saban spoke, and when he finished his comments, both men were requested to stand for photos with the trophy. Each briefly looked at the other but never at the same time as they readied for photos. They would soon be on their separate ways, and Harbaugh would return to his team. The routine that night wouldn't vary from any other before a game. There would be a movie, and he planned to talk to the players.

"Kind of get the red blood pumping a little bit so you can visualize it," he said. "Then go to sleep and see how good of a night's sleep you can get. Sometimes you do, sometimes you don't. We really stressed a good night's sleep last night. Kind of feel like that's the sleep you play on. Got a darned good one last night. Anything tonight will just be a bonus. Wake up tomorrow, and everybody has their own approach to game day. J.J. has one, other guys have a different approach. Just going to have to go through our routine and then get to the stadium, and then it's like new. You're in a new setting, and it takes five or ten minutes to adjust. But at some point you've got to lock in and you've got to get the rhythm. Rhythm, get the rhythm, get the freaking rhythm, and then toe meets leather and it's on. I never worry about our guys once the game starts because I know that they're going to react and do what they do and do it really well. Yeah, can't wait for that moment. Can't wait to watch our guys compete in this game."

It was finally game day, New Year's Day with beautiful weather and a cloudless blue sky. Michigan players said they knew what they had to get done to win and advance for a run at the biggest prize in college football.

"The most important two things we need to do is start fast," Corum said. "In a big game like this, you can't get behind the eight ball. You must start fast whether that be the first or second drive, but points have to get put up early, and the defense needs to make stops. Start fast I would say is No. 1, and No. 2 in a game like this, you can't make mistakes. You have to make sure the other team makes more mistakes than you in terms of penalties and things like that. We have to make sure we pay attention to details, we're precise, and we make no mistakes because mistakes can kill you."

Hours before kickoff, the Michigan players began to emerge from the tunnel outside their locker room and make their way onto the field. The Rose Bowl setting is breathtaking with the backdrop of the San Gabriel Mountains, and they were taking it in and getting a feel for the environment. Corum, who arrived at the stadium wearing a Barry Sanders No. 20 Pro Bowl jersey, took his time making his way to the field. He reached the mouth of the tunnel, looked up at the stadium, and then stared downward for a while clearly soaking in the moment. Zinter walked onto the field on crutches. He wouldn't be playing, but his presence there meant everything to him and to his teammates. As the players headed back to the locker room before returning for pregame warmups, they stopped to sign autographs and take selfies with young Michigan fans.

Michigan was on offense to open the game, and McCarthy, who threw those two costly pick-sixes in the semifinal loss to TCU a year earlier, appeared to throw an interception on the game's first play. The call was overturned on a replay review. "I was expecting to get chewed out, but with Coach Harbaugh, it was just, 'Hey, man, it's good you got that out of your system, let's roll out,'" McCarthy said.

Harbaugh met McCarthy on the sideline after the first series and spoke calmly to his quarterback. "First play of the game, he's clearly throwing the ball away, and I can tell you having made a bad play in a football game, it's like a train going through your head," Harbaugh said. "I mean, you see red. It's like a deafening siren. There's a lot of guys that will hang their head and go in the tank or get that deer-in-the-headlights look, but every guy that had that happen to them in our game came back and made a phenomenal play."

Both teams went three-and-out their first possession, but things quickly changed when Morgan, the Michigan freshman who had made his debut returning punts a game earlier against Iowa in the Big Ten championship, muffed a return recovered by Alabama. Four plays later, the Tide had a 7–0 lead.

"I think that first five minutes of the game, everybody had like a, 'Oh, shit, here we go again,'" Keegan said. "But once we make a play, we get momentum going, our offense is dangerous."

Michigan responded with an impressive 10-play, 75-yard touchdown drive that included a 21-yard run by Corum and a 19-yard completion to running back Kalel Mullings. Corum would score on an eight-yard pass from McCarthy to tie the game.

In the second quarter, McCarthy connected with Tyler Morris on a 38-yard touchdown, but the extra point was missed as the Wolverines took a 13–7 lead. On Alabama's final drive of the first half, the Tide reached the Michigan 25-yard line, but Milroe, who had been swarmed by the Wolverines' defenders, took his fifth sack for a seven-yard loss that forced them to settle for a field goal and trailed 13–10 at halftime.

The teams traded punts in the third quarter, but Alabama was driving as the game moved into the fourth quarter and took a 17–13 lead in the opening seconds. Two Michigan possessions later, James Turner would miss on a 49-yard field-goal attempt. Alabama would expand its lead to 20–13 on a 52-yard field goal with 4:41 left in the game.

Michigan began from its 25-yard line and would face fourth-and-2 from its own 33.

"I looked at the guys and I said, 'This is our last drive together,'" Keegan said.

"Big up to Trevor Keegan," Wilson said. "He kept telling us, 'We get a first down and it's going to roll,' and he was right."

McCarthy found Corum on the right side with a short pass, and he took off for a 27-yard gain, but a block in the back called against Roman Wilson would negate 10 yards. Michigan had the ball at midfield instead of at the Alabama 40-yard line. McCarthy then ran for 16 yards and, on the next play, connected with Wilson for a 29-yard gain. Two plays later, Wilson scored on a four-yard pass from McCarthy to tie the game with 1:34 left. They had gone 75 yards in just over three minutes.

"It was one of those games I had to keep my head in the game, keep going," Wilson said. "I kept telling myself, 'Bro, be ready, be ready.' I made a bad play and the guys had to pick me up and I had to make it up for them."

The Tide gained a first down on its final drive in regulation, but three straight incompletions from Milroe forced a punt. Seemed like a routine conclusion to regulation, but on the return, Jake Thaw muffed the punt at the Michigan 6-yard line and recovered at the 1-yard line as three Alabama players converged on him to avoid a disastrous conclusion.

"The way he handled it and not freaking out once the ball was going towards the end zone and accidentally kicking it or muffing it again and making sure he didn't fumble it when he got hit by those three guys," McCarthy said. "There's a lot of good that he did in that scary situation that I feel like needs to be appreciated."

It was the last of several special-teams errors in the game: the two muffed punt returns, a bad snap on a missed extra point by always-steady long-snapper William Wagner, and the missed field goal by Turner.

"I made the biggest mistake of my life on the biggest stage of my life," Thaw said. "It hurts, but I'm not wavering in confidence. When I saw the ball off the foot, I really thought it was going to land right at the 10, right where I was standing," Thaw said. "As it got closer, my last adjustments took me back. If I could do all over again, I would have run forward and bluffed away from the ball. Once I didn't, just obviously, okay, secure the football. Strike two. Now it's two mistakes I've made in one play. So just try to do everything I can to not make a bad play worse. I was just lucky I was able to get on the football. I owe a lot of thanks to Coach Moore, and I owe a lot of thanks to that offensive line for getting us off the goal line and going out there and winning that football game."

With 44 seconds left in regulation, Michigan was able to get out of trouble and send the game to overtime. The Wolverines got the opening possession and the offense went on. Corum went eight yards on the first play and then 17 up the middle for a touchdown and a 27–20 lead.

"He was not going to be denied," Michigan running backs coach Mike Hart said after the game of Corum's touchdown. "That's what I told [the coaches on the headset], just give [No.] 2 the ball. If you give 2 the ball, we'll be fine. He's a dog. Give him the ball."

"I don't know what happened when he scored, I just heard it," Keegan said. "He's just a special guy. You could see there's something in his eyes. He was going to get everything done. He was gonna get it in there for us."

Now it was up to the Michigan defense, a role it relished. These players wanted to be known as finishers, and that's what they did. On second-and-9, Milroe rushed up the middle to the Michigan 9-yard line. Two plays later, Mason Graham stuffed Jase McClellan for a five-yard loss, and the Tide faced third down and goal from the 14. An 11-yard gain made it fourth down at the Michigan 3-yard line. Michigan called timeout, then Alabama took a timeout. Milroe rushed up the middle but was stuffed for a one-yard gain by Derrick Moore.

"We were playing Cover 0," Colson said. "Coach was telling us all the time this is the moment we were built for. This is the moment we come out here to play for. We knew exactly what was going to happen. When the moment gets tough, you go to your best player, and they went to their best player, and we were right there to stop it. We said it's fourth down, one last play, everybody strained, everybody strained to the ball."

The Michigan sideline began to go crazy, and the players rushed the field to celebrate, maize and blue confetti flying. McCarthy found a rose to clench between his teeth, a trophy like no other, while others kept running around and rejoicing with teammates.

Former Michigan tight end Jake Butt, a captain in 2016 who was at the Rose Bowl working for the Big Ten Network, couldn't help himself. He wasn't scheduled to go on air immediately and found himself caught up in the emotion. He sprinted up and down the field hugging and cheering the players.

"When we went back on air, I put my suit on and we were good to go," said Butt, who had been drenched in sweat. "It was worth it, though. I made some great memories. I kept screaming and saying, 'One more, one more, one more!' I tried to take it all in. That's almost an indescribable feeling. You're always part of Michigan. You always share in the joy of victory and the pain of loss if you played there. If you're part of the Michigan family, you are part of it to different extents. But of course, when you're part of it in terms of practicing and sacrificing every day, nothing will ever compare to that. I feel part of this in the sense that I feel like I know these guys and I have a good relationship with a lot of them. They're just awesome, high-character people and I'm blown away by how they carry themselves."

Jansen, who had won at the Rose Bowl on New Year's Day in 1998 and became a national champion that day, watched the final defensive stop, and while his radio partner, Doug Karsch, called the play, Jansen erupted with two long exclamations, drawing out a "Yeah!" and another as long as he could.

"One of the false narratives that has gone around the last few years is the '97 wants to remain the only national champion," Jansen said. "The final play of the broadcast, the excitement I had was echoed by every single guy on the '97 team. We have been starved for a national championship. We want more national titles. We want more guys to experience exactly what we've had."

Michigan would have that opportunity a week later in Houston, but in this moment, in one of college football's most beautiful settings, the Wolverines kept alive their "natty or bust" momentum.

"This is a game I've dreamed about since high school, since I committed here just like everybody else," Wilson said. "Just all the work, all the grind, all those long days, all the tough days, all the adversity, everything this team had to deal with and overcame, it all showed up in this game. This team's amazing. I can't stop saying I'm so proud of this team for what we've built. I hope it stays a long time."

Keegan sat on the trainer's table and was getting the tape cut off his feet and ankles. He was stunned that despite the mistakes the Wolverines had made in the game, they would be heading to Houston to play for a national championship. "I have no idea how we won that game," Keegan said. "We left four points on the board. But we have guys who rally around each other. We've been through so much and we're kinda just used to this moment."

Harbaugh raised his arms the moment he saw Moore make the stop.

"Glorious," Harbaugh said of the win. "It was right where we wanted to be. It's everything that we worked for, everything that we prepared for, everything we hoped for, everything we trained and strained for. The team was just not going to be denied. J.J. said it when he walked off this same podium last year in the semifinal game. He said, we're going to be back. What he told me was not only are we going to be back, we're going to win. And there he did and in overtime against Alabama, I think the last quarterback to win in overtime against Alabama was none other than Tom Brady. I've said it before, but right here, this is the greatest quarterback in University of Michigan [history]. In a college career there's been nobody at Michigan better than J.J. I know we talk about it, an amalgamation of quarterbacks. He is that guy."

The Rose Bowl overtime game was watched by 27.2 million viewers, according to ESPN, the largest college football audience since 28.4 million watched the Alabama-Georgia national championship in 2018. The game had a peak viewership of 32.8 million, best of any CFP semifinal. Washington's Sugar Bowl semifinal against Texas averaged 18.4 million. Michigan had been part of the two most-viewed college games of the season, including the Michigan–Ohio State game with 19.1 million viewers.

A few days after the semifinal, Corum would share that he didn't want to dwell too much on the big win in the Rose Bowl so that he'd remain laser-focused on the ultimate prize. He had made the promise way back in February during a basketball game that Michigan would win it all, and the Rose Bowl was a great win, but just the next step.

"It was always for us Houston or bust," Corum said. "We haven't done it yet, so have to stay locked in this week. The hay is never in the barn. Make sure we watch as much film as we can over the next couple days and make sure we're prepared for [the national title game]. This is everything I dreamed of, everything I came back for. Just blessed to be here."

And now it was on to Houston to attempt to fulfill those dreams.

– 14 –

PLAYING FOR THE
NATIONAL CHAMPIONSHIP

AFTER winning the Rose Bowl, Michigan immediately began preparing for Washington, a 37–31 winner over Texas in the Sugar Bowl CFP semifinal, which would be a matchup of No. 1 versus No. 2 in the national championship. Long before the outcomes of the semifinal games, Michigan coaches had already been studying Kalen DeBoer's Huskies and prolific left-handed quarterback Michael Penix Jr., the Heisman Trophy runner-up, so this was not some sort of final-exam cramming.

The Wolverines knew on December 3, after the College Football Playoff final four was announced, that if they beat Alabama and advanced, they would play either Texas or Washington in the title game. Staff members began film breakdowns in preparation for either possibility. But after the Rose Bowl, once Michigan touched down in Ann Arbor on the flight from Los Angeles, they switched to a precision focus on the Huskies. It would be a quick turnaround with six days between games. The previous year, Georgia and TCU had eight days between the semifinals and national championship game.

"We decided to fly right back after the game in Pasadena," Harbaugh said. "Felt like it saved us some hours, get back to Ann Arbor, get rest in our own beds."

Harbaugh liked the idea of trying to keep to a normal game-week schedule, and this plan would allow for that. It had been about a month since the players had adhered to a typical in-season schedule, considering the large gap between the Big Ten championship and CFP semifinal, but with a team full of veterans, it was effortless getting back to the grind.

Washington, meanwhile, played the late CFP semifinal in New Orleans and waited to fly back to Seattle on Tuesday, January 2, after DeBoer decided it would be best for the players to spend the night in the Big Easy. His staff, however, returned to campus immediately after the game.

During the brief layover in Ann Arbor before the Wolverines flew to Houston on Friday ahead of Monday night's national championship game, Harbaugh spoke midweek to media about the team's miscues in the 27–20 overtime win over Alabama in the Rose Bowl and was clearly making a point. Yes, the Tide challenged the Wolverines, but Michigan had been in several pressure situations of their own making, mistakes that could have been costly.

Harbaugh, by laying this out there, wanted to flip the narrative. It wasn't really about all the mistakes made, it was about how the Wolverines steadied themselves and responded. Steve Clinkscale, Michigan's co–defensive coordinator/defensive backs coach, earlier in the season had talked to the team the night before the Big Ten opener against Rutgers about how to respond to adversity. Never flinch, he told them. For Harbaugh, the Rose Bowl was the absolute perfect example of how the Wolverines didn't give in to the moment and never flinched.

"The things that jump out are just how we responded in the pressure moments, in the pressure times—offense, defense, special teams—and rose to the occasion," Harbaugh told media two days after the Rose Bowl. "Tremendous play during the pressure moments of the game."

Everyone knew all of the miscues, starting with the first play of the game when McCarthy threw an apparent interception that was reversed by officials. There was a bad snap by usually sure-handed long-snapper William Wagner on a missed extra point; the missed field goal by Turner; the block-in-the-back penalty against Wilson on a 35-yard play from Corum; and two muffed punts, the first by Morgan and the second by Thaw in the final seconds of regulation after Michigan had tied the game, which could have made for a disastrous finish for the Wolverines.

Any one of those plays could have derailed a less mature team's demeanor and snowballed to the point of no return for Michigan. For all the talk of Michigan's lack of competition in the nonconference schedule and how the Wolverines coasted through October essentially untested, the regular-season games in November against Purdue, on the road against Penn State and Maryland and then home against Ohio State took the competition up a notch, especially for Michigan's offense, and they were tests that made the team tougher.

"I just kind of feel like those pressure situations are what make teams great," defensive tackle Mason Graham said of the Rose Bowl mistakes.

Much of the talk heading into the Rose Bowl was about Milroe, Alabama's quarterback, and the threat he presented defenses. As Michigan prepared for the national title game against Washington, facing Penix became the hot topic. Edge rusher Jaylen Harrell described the lefty, who was not completely unfamiliar to Michigan since he had played at Indiana, as the best passer they'd face all season. He singled out his quick release and the fact he didn't get hit or sacked much playing behind the Huskies' Joe Moore Award–winning offensive line.

But this matchup was just as much about McCarthy, who had helped direct the Wolverines through an unbeaten season and was still stinging from the loss at TCU in the Fiesta Bowl CFP semifinal the year before. McCarthy could not allow himself to forget his two pick-sixes in the 51–45 defeat, after which he stood alone, helmet in hand, and watched the Horned Frogs celebrate, purple confetti falling across the field. It was similar to the moment he experienced a year before that when the Wolverines lost to eventual national champion Georgia in the Orange Bowl CFP semifinal. McCarthy, then a freshman, wasn't the starter but did play toward the end of the game and still deeply felt the hurt as he stood with fellow freshmen Donovan Edwards and Andrel Anthony, as well as Corum, no one speaking a word to each other as they watched the Bulldogs celebrate.

McCarthy headed into national championship game week coming off yet another similar postgame, on-field experience, this time as the victor. After the Wolverines' 27–20 overtime victory against No. 4 Alabama in the Rose Bowl semifinal, he walked onto the field in front of the end zone with Alabama emblazoned in white on a crimson background. McCarthy got in a crouch then bowed his head and soaked in the moment. This is what victory felt like. After experiencing the pain of defeat the last two years, he wanted to embrace those emotions. "Those moments, I cherish every single one of them, win or loss, just because you work so hard every single day throughout the off-season, during the season, to get to points like that," McCarthy said. "Just taking it in, win or loss, is just always something that I really just appreciate.

"This past one, it was just—all the extra work and all the different things that I did this past off-season and this season, just like reflecting back on those [things] and how hard I pushed myself and training seven to eight times a week and going to the separate trainer where we would do these conditioning days and I'm throwing up 75 percent of the time down there. Just all the extra things that I did, just kind of taking that all in on the field and just realizing, 'Hey, it was worth every single second of pain that I went through, and I would do it all over again if I had the choice.'"

Greg Holcomb, a private quarterback coach who founded Next Level Athletix Quarterback Training, has known McCarthy since he was a smallish sixth-grader. He knew the first time he saw McCarthy throw that the kid was special. "He's physically gifted beyond almost any kid that I've ever seen," he said. "When he threw a football for the first time, I said to him, 'I don't know if I've seen a sixth-grader throw a football like that.'"

Fast forward to McCarthy's junior season at Michigan and plenty of people had taken notice of his arm despite the fact Michigan's offense isn't pass heavy. Harbaugh had already crowed before the Rose Bowl that McCarthy was, in his opinion, NFL ready. But still, heading into the national title game, it felt like McCarthy was flying a bit low under the radar while Penix garnered the attention.

This was of little concern to McCarthy, who never expressed interest in personal accolades. Even earlier in the season when his name came up in the Heisman Trophy conversation, while he appreciated the attention, he certainly wasn't seeking it. "I've never been about [it]," he said in those days before the national championship game. "I've always been someone that chases purpose, not fame. I could care less what the media says about me or the light they put me in. All I really care about is winning football games. At the end of the day, it's about winning football games no matter what it takes, and I could care less what comes of it, what other people think about me or what they [think of] me amongst the other quarterbacks in this class right now. All I care about is winning games."

One of the reasons Harbaugh and McCarthy clicked and, perhaps, why it seemed McCarthy's play dipped while his coach was sidelined for those final three regular-season games during his suspension, is that Harbaugh played quarterback at Michigan and at the highest level in the NFL. They spoke the same quarterback language, and sometimes, nothing had to be said between the two. What Harbaugh saw from McCarthy in the Rose Bowl and dealing with pressure moments was complete calm, and he had been tested from the get-go with the overturned interception.

Harbaugh had thrown an interception or two in his career and understood. But he focused on how well McCarthy had bounced back from the early mistake. "How about the one-handed catch [McCarthy] made on the trick play," Harbaugh said, "the throwback, and then he turns, wheels, and throws the ball? There was just a ton of great plays made in pressure."

Campbell, in his first season as quarterbacks coach, also saw from McCarthy in that game and, really, all season, an ability to never get rattled and to always keep his emotions in check. Throughout the Rose Bowl game, Campbell reminded McCarthy to never get caught up in the ups and downs and stay zoned in on a one-play-at-a-time approach.

"You can let all the emotion out at the end of the game," Campbell told him.

And that's exactly what McCarthy was doing on the Rose Bowl field alone after the game, taking it all in, letting out all the emotion. He felt a sense of accomplishment getting Michigan over the semifinal hump but knew there was much more work to do. A national championship was in reach and, yeah, maybe everyone was talking about Penix and the high-powered Washington pass offense, but McCarthy was supremely confident in his ability to lead the Wolverines' offense.

While the coaches and players and staff were preparing for the enormous stage at Houston's NRG Stadium, former Michigan players, many on the 1997 undefeated team that won the AP national championship, the program's last national title, were either making the journey to Texas or they were enjoying this special ride from their homes. In 1997 the Wolverines went 12–0, including a win over Washington State at the Rose Bowl. The AP title would go to Michigan that year, while the coaches voted for Nebraska as national champions. The players on that 1997 team, like Michigan fans, were hungry for another national championship.

"We have been waiting for 26 years to welcome another Michigan football team in the most exclusive...fraternity within Michigan football," said Eric Mayes, a co-captain in 1997. "It was a mountaintop experience. And that mountain has been the foundation that I've used for the rest of my life. That foundation, the lessons, the relationships, the spirit, being a champion, has walked with me and been a part of me ever since."

Chris Howard was a standout running back on that team and James Hall a defensive lineman in 1997, and the two communicate all the time. Shortly after the 2023 Wolverines defeated Ohio State, Hall texted Howard and praised the current team. That was notable, Howard said, because Hall is not one to readily offer compliments.

"He said, 'In my opinion, this is the best football team in Michigan's history,'" Howard said, reading from a text message Hall had sent. "Their mental and emotional fortitude allowed them to navigate situations where the adults in the room egregiously failed them. Despite immense pressure and distractions, they remained steadfast and overcame adversity, which is beyond impressive and deserves acknowledgment.'"

Braylon Edwards, the great receiver from Michigan, said this run to the national championship and this team made him "fall in love" with Michigan again and restored the magic that drew him to the football program in the first place when he was a kid. Devin Gardner, a former Michigan quarterback who grew up in the area, went through tough seasons as a player but also as a fan. Former players, once their playing days conclude, become fans and share the fan experience of riding the roller coaster of highs and lows. The last three seasons—especially 2023, for the fans, including Gardner, provided a unique experience, a return to the top of college football and a chance to win it all.

"I've never seen Michigan football like this," Gardner said. "You think about '97—I wasn't watching football then. I was five or six. By the time I even started watching football, about 10 years old, Michigan football wasn't dominant like this, and Ohio State had Heisman Trophy winners and they were really amazing. I've never seen this version of Michigan football. Obviously, the history of Michigan football tells you how dominant Michigan has been, most wins and all that stuff, but I've never experienced that. I've never experienced Michigan going into a game knowing they're going to win every single time and if they get their back against the wall, they'll be able to respond. I've never seen that version. As a player, we thought we would win every single time, but if I was a fan of my teams and Denard Robinson's teams, I wouldn't be so sure that we're going to win."

Jansen, who was such a big part of the 1997 national title team also felt a connection to the current team because of his work as radio analyst and handling all the interviews with players and coaches on the in-house podcasts the athletics department produces. Although he spoke to the team before the Rose Bowl about the mystique of that venue and the importance of the College Football Playoff semifinal game against Alabama, he also took the opportunity to advance the conversation and talked to the players about what it means to be in the rarefied air of a national champion. What he found from their response is that learning about his history and that of the '97 team and applying it to making their own history did matter to them. They asked him questions to know how that moment might feel and learned that while maybe those immediate emotions may never be recaptured, the enormity of always being able to call themselves national champions will remain forever.

After a final practice in Ann Arbor, the Wolverines arrived the afternoon of January 5, a Friday, at George Bush Intercontinental Airport on a 747-400, known as the "Queen of the Skies." The team traveled in style, transported on the enormous plane with a customized interior. Players, coaches, staff, and family members disembarked on mobile stairways connected to two exits, and perhaps most notable was seeing Zak Zinter, five weeks after surgery on his left leg, walking without the use of crutches.

Before a bevy of reporters and television cameras gathered on the tarmac, Harbaugh beamed. "Exactly where we wanted to be," he said. "Right where we hoped we would be. Our guys have worked so hard to get here."

Harbaugh praised Washington and rattled off all the Huskies' positives—their quarterback play, their offensive line, the receivers, their athleticism in the defensive secondary. No weaknesses, he said. Harbaugh certainly wasn't going to share anything negative or controversial, because there is no gain in such an approach, but he also made clear his team was ready for anything and offered a familiar refrain: that to be the best, you've got to beat the best.

Those airport arrival news conferences are not meant to be anything more than a few sound bites, photos, and videos of the players, but Harbaugh conveyed immense confidence in those few moments. "Our guys are very focused on making it all the way," he said before the team departed for its hotel.

Unlike the lead-up to the Rose Bowl—a month between the conference championships and CFP semifinal—which allowed for weeks of stories, the short turnaround to the national title game left less time for storylines to develop. One, however, was a constant at the media day in Houston on Saturday when every player and coach from both teams appeared at separate times. The leadoff question to Harbaugh wasn't about his team but his future and whether the outcome of the game would affect his interest in returning to the NFL. "I have no idea about that. I couldn't be more happy to be here," Harbaugh said. "This is a tremendous city. They do everything big in Texas, and this is cool. This is right where we want to be. This is why we worked. To get here."

That wasn't enough. Question No. 2 at his podium interview time was whether he had assured anyone at Michigan he would return for a 10ᵗʰ season. Harbaugh had been asked about his coaching future so many times over the years, this one in particular, that it became more interesting to see how he would find various ways to address or deflect it. Among his stock techniques was to take a question, then distract with a response that had little to do with what he was asked. This time, in an effort to move along the question-and-answer session, Harbaugh pointed out that there's a calendar. "I'll gladly talk about the future next week," he said. "And I hope to have one, how about that? A future, I hope to have one. Yes. Thank you."

At a national championship, national media are in abundance. Sure, there were a number of national media members at the Rose Bowl, but they were split among the CFP semifinals—some in Pasadena and some in New Orleans. At the national title game in Houston, however, everyone who covers college football on a national level was in attendance.

With that in mind, the national spotlight shined on Penix, although it wasn't like McCarthy was being ignored. At 6'3", 213 pounds, Penix had been electrifying during the season and, entering this final game, directed the nation's top passing offense, averaging 350 yards a game. On the flip side, Michigan's defense, coordinated by Minter, was the nation's best in two categories, total and scoring defense. The Wolverines were yielding an average of 243.1 yards and 10.2 points per game. This would be the No. 1 passing offense and against the No. 1 defense. As Harbaugh said, to be the best, you've got to beat the best.

To prepare Michigan's defense for Penix, backup Davis Warren, who had been battling a shoulder issue much of the season, took on the scout-team role of the Heisman Trophy runner-up despite being a righthander. Penix, entering the game, had completed 66.7 percent of his pass attempts for 4,648 yards and 35 touchdowns, against nine interceptions. Warren had been tasked with trying to reproduce Penix's style at quarterback to prepare Michigan's defense.

He joked that he hadn't yet mastered the ability to throw as a left-hander but had studied Penix's tendencies and how he would get rid of the ball. Warren worked on escaping to his left to give the defense a better look. He felt confident in his ability to help the defense prepare and believed Michigan would be able to stop the dynamic quarterback.

This game wasn't solely about Penix, of course. Michigan's run game, particularly Blake Corum and the promise of Donovan Edwards returning to the form that distinguished his performances at the end of the 2022 season, were highlighted. While the Wolverines still considered themselves what Sherrone Moore dubbed a year earlier, a "smash" offense, physical in the run game behind a tough-blocking offensive line, this offense had different layers. The offensive line had earned the Joe Moore Award the previous two seasons, but the 2023 line had to do some shuffling, mostly because of injuries, throughout the season, and Edwards had not been the back he had been projected to be at the start of the season. This was not lost on Edwards, who discussed his challenging season at the national title game media day and shared that he sought the assistance of a therapist during the season to help with his mental health. And while McCarthy was coming off a three-touchdown performance against Alabama, in four of the five games before that, he didn't have a touchdown pass.

With all of that in mind, it felt like this game was boiling down to Penix versus the Michigan defense. Which is exactly how the

Michigan defenders liked it, especially the front seven. "One of the best quarterbacks I've seen play ball," Harrell said. "We've gotta find ways to disrupt him as a passer, because he gets the ball off quick. We'll have some things dialed up. He has a quick release, but there are other ways to get in his way, getting him off his spot, still hitting him, getting pressure on him, just making him feel your presence all game. That will be key to this game for us."

Penix had talented receivers to work with, including Rome Odunze, who was entering the title game with a school-record 1,553 receiving yards and had caught 13 touchdown passes. He would be a test for Michigan cornerback Will Johnson, but it didn't seem as much a game about the Wolverines' secondary as it did about the guys up front.

"This is the most challenging team we've faced this season," Elston, Michigan's defensive-line coach said. "Their offensive line is very talented. They've only given up 11 sacks this season. We need to affect the quarterback. We may not get him on the ground in terms of a sack, but we need to affect him, gotta prevent him from getting out and hurting us with scrambles. The front seven is critical."

Michigan sacked Milroe six times in the Rose Bowl, including five in the first half, and no one was anticipating those numbers against Penix. But one of the Wolverines' four defensive pillars is ball disruption, which can prove just as costly, as evidenced by the fact that Michigan was No. 2 nationally in turnover margin. What had helped the Michigan defense all season was the ability to rotate players along the front, so they tended to be fresh when they'd get into a game.

This wasn't a group with a player like edge rusher Aidan Hutchinson, whose 14 single-season sacks set a Michigan record in 2021. Hutchinson, a Heisman runner-up, would be selected No. 2 overall in the NFL Draft by Detroit in 2022. In this defense, the statistics were spread around. Minter designed his scheme this way and instilled an all-for-one, one-for-all approach.

"We're not selfish. Everybody eats," Wolverines defensive tackle Kenneth Grant said. "Coach Minter calls it an 'everybody eats' defense or a 'no star' defense. We want to be the best defense in the country, and not one person can just do that. We've all got to do that to be the best defense. There's not one person being selfish."

It certainly wasn't a new concept, of course, but it's one that isn't always easy to embrace. For the Michigan defensive players, though, it was all about what they'd call doing their "one of 11," each player doing their job to fulfill the goal of the 11 as a unit.

"That's been a big thing for us," defensive end Braiden McGregor said. "We have it schemed up that if everybody does their job, the offenses can't succeed. Being able to do our one-11, with our front playing as well as we play and the linebackers being so unselfish, to be able to fit any gap, to be able to pull off double-teams for us, it just flows through the whole defense. And obviously we have great [defensive backs] covering who still want to come down and smack the running backs, smack the quarterbacks. So I think the defense as a whole, the competition, and how much love we have for each other is a big thing for us."

With the pressure from the athletic defensive line going after, in this case, Penix, opportunities would be created for the linebackers, who entered the game occupying the top three spots in tackles on the team. "It all starts on the front line," linebacker Michael Barrett said. "We have to knock out the run early, get to the quarterback early, have to get him uncomfortable. We're definitely counting on those guys, same as we're counting on the DBs to handle it downfield. The way we jell together, the way we work together. We work day-in and day-out, and that's why I think the D-line is so dominant. And the freaking monsters we have over there, we have some dudes."

The defense had come up big all season, especially the last portion of the season, and it was ready to control the game against Washington.

On the eve of the biggest game in college football, Harbaugh and DeBoer sat together at a final news conference, both looking at ease and smiling. Harbaugh had coached in a Super Bowl when he was head coach of the San Francisco 49ers, but this was the national championship, coaching his alma mater.

"It would mean so much for our players, for them to know what it's like to be champions, just be simply referred to as 'national champions.' And for their parents to have their son be a champion, a national champion, for their grandparents to have a grandson, for their brothers and sisters to have a brother who is a national champion," Harbaugh said during that final pregame news conference. "What it would mean to me? For my kids to know their dad is a national champion, and for my parents and my brother and my sister. That's the overwhelming thing, just that so many people would be able to enjoy that, be a part of that. For my wife, for her husband to be a national champion. For me, not so much, but for everybody else, yeah, that would be huge."

Harbaugh managed to sidestep yet again a question about NFL speculation. He was asked if this was his last time coaching the Wolverines, what did he plan to say as a farewell message to the team before they took the field Monday night? Harbaugh didn't fall for the underlying trap. "My message to our guys is going to be play as hard as you can, as fast as you can, as long as you can, and don't worry. And just go have at it," he said, redirecting his response away from the question. "It's been a group of guys that I've had to pull them back at times. Have never had to talk them into anything. And I just can't wait. I can't wait to watch them compete, watch them have at it. That's going to be my overwhelming feeling, let's just go, let it rip.

And we're going to have to play well. This is a tremendous, tremendous team that we're playing. Just thorough in every way."

Earlier on Monday, the day of the national title game, the team hotel was buzzing. Michigan fans had gathered to send off the team and clogged the lobby. It was loud, festive. Upstairs, some of Michigan's biggest donors had met for a private event to raise funds for the athletics department's Name, Image, and Likeness (NIL) Champions Circle. University of Michigan president Santa Ono and athletics director Warde Manuel stopped in to rally for the cause. What better opportunity to encourage donations than the Wolverines' first appearance in the championship game in the College Football Playoff format that began in 2014? Everyone seemed to be soaking up the atmosphere. Meanwhile, at a nearby Hampton Inn in downtown Houston, a large group of players from the 1997 Michigan team gathered for a three-hour "Pep Rally" and joined in to send off the team to NRG Stadium.

While it was festive inside, bad weather was brewing, the sky a dark gray with reports of a tornado watch. Michigan arrived at the stadium hours before kickoff. Harbaugh, carrying a blue Michigan duffel, led the way to the locker room, his coaching staff not far behind. Corum was the first of the players to make his way into the bowels of NRG Stadium and looked every part of a Texan, wearing a big black cowboy hat and a big Texas-style belt buckle with light blue jeans. Everything is bigger in Texas, as the saying goes, and Corum was embracing his environment.

Not long after their arrival, in the hours before kickoff, Michigan players took the field, some working together, throwing and catching passes, while others found individual space. Keegan, the left guard, was off to one sideline, working in a small area on footwork and explosive movements. Defensive tackles Jenkins and Grant went through some stretching and worked on drills designed for coming off the ball. It had started raining hard outside the closed stadium, and water leaked from a room onto a portion of the field where the Michigan players were, but no one seemed to mind. McCarthy walked onto the field three hours before kickoff and went through his pregame meditation. He sat crossed-legged in front of the goal post in the north end zone, his hat pulled low, his hoodie over his head, eyes closed, and spent the next 15 minutes finding his balance. Not long after, he began his warm-ups, with Harbaugh, wearing black receiver gloves, to McCarthy's left, catching passes and tossing the ball to his quarterback to warm up.

Finally, it was kickoff. Michigan started strong in the first quarter with 229 yards, including 174 rushing. Edwards gave the Wolverines an enormous boost, much like he had late in the 2022 season at Ohio State and in the Big Ten title game, and scored twice, on runs of 41 and 46 yards. In the final play just before the end of the quarter, Corum had a 59-yard run. Michigan's run game was clearly working and had that "smash" feel, as the Wolverines built a 14–3 lead.

"I was so excited for Donovan because I just felt like he needed that," Corum would later say about Edwards' dynamic first quarter. "He's back. Dono is back. That's something Donovan was praying for. He talked to the media the other day, [and] I listened to the interview. He said he's working on growing. He said he went to a therapist and just talking and talking. But Donovan, he puts in the work. He's always there."

The Huskies' defense stiffened, and Michigan's offensive production dipped, but the Wolverines, who never trailed in the game, led 17–10 at halftime. Each team had a field goal in the third quarter, after which Michigan led 20–13.

"We started fast," Corum said. "They slowed us up a little bit. But when we needed to start fast again, we started fast. They had us for a little bit. We knew they were going to get theirs."

Michigan held that seven-point lead when it began a fourth-quarter drive with 9:44 left from its 29-yard line. On the first play, McCarthy found tight end Colston Loveland for 41 yards to the Washington 30-yard line. Four plays later, Corum scored for the first time in the game on a 12-yard run, his 26th rushing touchdown of the season, with 7:09 left in the game.

Penix had been intercepted at the start of the second half by Will Johnson and now faced fourth-and-13 at the Michigan 30-yard line with 3:53 left. He was picked off for the second time, this time by Mike Sainristil, who returned it 81 yards to the Washington 8-yard line.

"I just knew I made a key play in the game," Sainristil said. "The guys up front forced Penix to overthrow it. All season long we've been saying tips and overthrows, we've got to get those. To be able to capitalize, and bringing the ball within the 10, give the offense a short field to work with, and they were able to go ahead and punch it in. We knew we won the game, but we also had the mindset that it's not over. Come back, get them off the field again, and let the offense do the deal."

Michigan's two-play drive culminated with Corum scoring again, this time from the 1-yard line with 3:37 left in the game. Washington would get the ball one last time and converted on fourth-and-1 to the Huskies' 31-yard line. Penix, however, would throw four straight incompletions. Michigan got the ball back with 1:49 left, ran three plays until time ticked off the clock, and claimed the Wolverines' first national championship in 26 years with a 34–13 victory.

"Coaches always say, playmakers have to make plays, and don't wait on anyone else to make a play," Corum said. "But today was a complete team effort. There's so many people making plays out there. And when we needed a play, someone made it, whether it had been myself or whether it had been Will or J.J. or Donovan, Colston. I could keep going on, just because so many guys made plays. But when the play needs to be made, playmakers make them. And we have a lot of them."

It meant the world to Michigan's top-rated defense to handle the test provided by Penix. He entered the game averaging 332 passing yards per game, but against the Wolverines he was 27-of-51 for 255 yards, with one touchdown, two interceptions, and one sack by Kenneth Grant.

"Man, we knew what time it was," Jaylen Harrell said of Michigan's defensive players. "We always love a challenge. It's the No. 1 offense, Joe Moore Award winners, and we had to come in here and prove we were the No. 1 defense in the country. And I think we did."

From the roof of NRG Stadium, maize and blue confetti mixed with white paper football shapes imprinted with "2024" and metallic gold streamers swirled in the air as they fell around the players and onto the field. Standing on a platform, Harbaugh gathered with much of the team as Queen's "We Are the Champions" blared from the speakers.

Harbaugh lifted the championship trophy with Corum to his right and Sainristil, holding a camera and beaming as he photographed the scene, to his left. McCarthy, Will Johnson, and Kris Jenkins were right behind him as Harbaugh looked over at Trevor Keegan motioning to his coach with his fist in the air before pulling it down multiple times. Harbaugh took the cue and announced to the crowd that his team was 15–0, "simply known as national champions." And as an exclamation point, he mimicked Keegan and with his right hand held high, he pulled it down and yelled, "Pull it down! Pull it down!"

Grant, the swift, athletic defensive tackle, basked in the moment and said reaching the goal proved something to anyone who questioned the Wolverines' hunger and abilities. "Michigan versus everybody," he said. "We've got that chip on our shoulder. Everybody says we're not good, but look at us now, we prevailed. Now everybody sees that we're good."

Did it vindicate Harbaugh and his program, which was scrutinized all season with two ongoing NCAA investigations? The players were asked in the postgame news conference about the off-field issues, and Harbaugh jumped in to answer. "We're innocent and we stood strong and tall because we knew we were innocent," he said. "And these guys are innocent. And overcome that? It wasn't that hard because we knew we were innocent. [The season] went exactly how we wanted it to go. It went exactly how we wanted it to go."

Harbaugh missed coaching six regular-season games because of two suspensions, and still the Wolverines were able to stay unbeaten.

"I'd say we came a long way, but in order to accomplish things like this, you've got to go to those dark places where everything's not great," McCarthy said. "And just the response, the urgency right after that last game last year [against TCU], it was different. I knew it. Just from being on the podium last year and saying we would be back. I knew the guys that were coming back. I had this feeling that it was going to be where we are right now. All the credit goes to the players on this team, everybody in that facility, Coach Harbaugh. That man, he's the reason we're here today."

Back in October during an appearance on the *Inside Michigan Radio* show, Harbaugh discussed how he didn't have any tattoos and then made a bold statement. "If we go undefeated, I'm going to get a 15–0 tattoo," he said. "Probably on the shoulder. And a Block M over it. I haven't configured the art yet, but if that happens, I will do it."

Well, it happened, and Harbaugh was pressed after the game about fulfilling that promise. "I said that I would get a tattoo," he said. "I have no ink on my body. No tattoos anywhere, but I did say that to our players. I said if we go 15–0, I'm getting a tattoo. It's 15–0. I'm going to put it on my shoulder, [but] I don't know if it's my left or right yet. I'm a right-handed quarterback, I'll probably get it on my right. And then an M, too, that's maize and blue. Also, that signifies a thousand in Roman numerals. Can't tell you what that means to us, too, that we reached a thousand wins this year."

Harbaugh would make good on his promise to get a tattoo on the morning of Michigan's spring game in April. He returned to Ann Arbor, along with several former coaches and players on the cusp of learning their NFL futures in the draft the next week, for a ring ceremony. The players and coaches were presented lacquer boxes that contained four rings: one for the Big Ten championship, another for the Rose Bowl, one from the College Football Playoff, and one for the national championship.

But there was other business to attend to. With two rings on his left hand and two on his right, Harbaugh sat down as Michigan-based tattoo artist Stephen Bateman created the tattoo on his upper right arm, a skinny Block M above "15–0."

"I'm impervious to pain," Harbaugh said, smiling while receiving the tattoo, the moment recorded in a video by Sainristil, who posted it to his Instagram story before the spring game on April 20. Once the tattoo was completed, Harbaugh looked down at his arm and smiled. "I can see, once you get one, you might want to start adding," he said, laughing. "I already want to put a rose on it."

Back on the field after the national championship game on January 8, players still lingered, some sharing time with family members who had moved to the first row of seats to be with them, others still sitting for postgame television interviews. Surrounded by a group of reporters, Manuel was getting quizzed about the potential of Harbaugh returning to the NFL. Manuel said he understood why NFL teams would want to talk to and potentially hire Harbaugh considering his blistering three-season run including the national title, not to mention the conference championship he won with the 49ers and the Super Bowl appearance.

"If I was in the pros, I would want to talk to him because of what he accomplished," Manuel said. "However, I'm not in the pros and

I want to keep him as our coach. I am proud that Jim is our coach. Doesn't matter what all the stuff that happened in the past, and it really doesn't matter what happens in the future. He's always gonna be somebody I'm proud of who coached the University of Michigan, who led this team, and if he decides he wants another opportunity to coach in the pros, then I'm going to be happy for him [but] sad for us, and we're going to move on and find the next person to lead. But I want him to stay at Michigan. I've said it, I believe it. Three, four years ago when people wanted me to get rid of him, I didn't because I believed in him then and I believe in him now."

Harbaugh's coaching future would become the focus of the next few weeks, but on the NRG Stadium field, maize and blue confetti everywhere, no one cared about anything but being national champions.

– 15 –

HARBUARY

THE LAST few years, January had become known, at least to those keeping an eye on the Michigan football program, as "Harbuary," roughly defined as the time in the new year shortly after the bowl game when it became anyone's guess what Harbaugh might do. Would he return for another season coaching his alma mater? Would he head back to the NFL, where he spent four seasons coaching the San Francisco 49ers and reached a Super Bowl and clearly coveted the thought of winning a Lombardi Trophy?

After winning a national championship and being on the ultimate of highs in college football, but also with two unresolved NCAA investigations and the threat of possible additional game suspensions ahead, perhaps this would be the right time for his departure. Understandably, this couldn't just be all about Harbaugh's hopes. There had to be an NFL team or two interested in the 60-year-old coach to make this a reality. But here he was in early Harbuary, at the peak in terms of his popularity and college coaching success after leading the Wolverines to the national title in early 2024. If he was ever going to be his most appealing to NFL teams, this would be the time.

There had been talk most of 2023 and particularly late in the season about Michigan locking down Harbaugh, getting him an extension so he could finish his coaching days in Ann Arbor. In October, Harbaugh said he wanted to feel wanted and said he felt that from Michigan. But there had also been the NFL rumors swirling, picking up steam in December as the Wolverines prepared for the Big Ten championship, and then they became more pronounced as they readied for the Rose Bowl CFP semifinal.

Not coincidentally, there also had been a shift in how Harbaugh handled NFL rumor talk. Before 2022, Harbaugh would routinely shoot down any NFL rumors that suggested he would make a return to the league. During the public Michigan football banquet in 2016 at the Laurel Manor in Livonia, Michigan, he assured the crowd he was sticking with the Wolverines. "I'm not leaving Michigan. Not even considering it," he told the crowd enthusiastically. "A lot of this talk is coming from our enemies, from coaches, you know the names. You probably know the names of the top three I'm referring to. They like to say that to the media. They like to tell that to the recruits, to their families, try to manipulate them into going to some other school besides Michigan. We know them as jive turkeys. Say it like it is. That's the way it is."

The "jive turkeys" reference immediately had the desired effect among the fan base and added to the aura he had developed since he arrived as he worked to get Michigan back on the map. Harbaugh had developed this reputation of being a bit zany with unusual recruiting visits that included a sleepover and a tree climb and challenging the NCAA rulebook by finding a loophole and going on a satellite camp tour. Later, he would take the team on overseas spring trips. Michigan players, their families, and fans would leave that night knowing Harbaugh wasn't going anywhere.

Two years later, he told ESPN's Adam Schefter that the NFL rumors were "a choreographed message" that he realized magically surfaced right around signing day. To that point, fanning the Harbaugh-to-the-NFL flames were all, at least in his opinion, about negative recruiting. "I'm on record right here, right now: I'm not going anywhere," Harbaugh told Schefter. "I'm staying at Michigan. We have big plans here, and there's a lot we want to accomplish."

In early 2020, the talk was all about a contract extension for Harbaugh, but with the COVID-19 pandemic, those discussions were shelved. Harbaugh entered the shortened season as the only Power Five coach with less than two years left on his original deal. Even that summer, when it was unclear if the Big Ten would have a season, Harbaugh was upbeat about his lack of an extension, saying there were "just other fish, bigger fish to fry."

Michigan would endure the 2–4 season, and Manuel, the athletics director who said he heard from plenty who thought he should fire Harbaugh, retained his head coach but at half the salary, slashing the original $8 million to $4 million. The contract was highly incentivized and perhaps sparked Harbaugh's competitiveness. Michigan would go on in 2021 to snap an eight-game losing streak against Ohio State, win the Big Ten championship, and earn a berth in the College Football Playoff semifinal, where the Wolverines lost to eventual national champion Georgia.

After that 2021 season, however, Harbaugh was no longer shooting down NFL rumors with "jive turkey" references. On February 2, 2022—national signing day—he flew to Minnesota and interviewed with the Vikings for their head-coaching position. He did not receive an offer, returned to Ann Arbor, and signed an extension with Michigan. Harbaugh would later reveal the thought of trying for a Super Bowl victory tugged at him, and he needed to explore the opportunity.

In early 2023, after another successful season, including a win at Ohio State, another Big Ten title, and another CFP berth, Harbaugh engaged in conversations with the Denver Broncos about the head-coaching vacancy there. That job would eventually go to Sean

Payton, and Harbaugh would remain at Michigan for his ninth and most successful season.

But things felt different in late December, especially because Harbaugh, who had never really worked with an agent, hired Don Yee, the high-powered agent with deep NFL ties. Long gone were the days of Harbaugh saying he wasn't going anywhere and suggesting rivals were planting rumors. If the two previous years had shown anything, it was his desire to listen to NFL teams. During the Rose Bowl welcome for Michigan and Alabama at Disneyland, Harbaugh faced questions about the NFL speculation that suggested he might entertain a return to the league, particularly to the nearby Los Angeles Chargers, a franchise for which he had played in 1999–2000.

If there was one thing that Harbaugh had sharpened during his years responding to the media covering Michigan, it was the ability to deflect and also to sidestep questions. He could filibuster with the best of them if he felt that was his best response, often taking his time answering a question by naming off practically every player on his roster. When he was asked at Disneyland abut the NFL, he responded in vintage Harbaugh fashion.

"Such a one-track mind. That's the way we're going about things," Harbaugh said, using a familiar refrain from the season and how the team approached each week. "Literally, whatever day we're in, looking to get the most out of it, dominate the day, then we're going to sleep tonight and wake up tomorrow and see if we can't dominate that day. It's a single-minded group. Just very focused on taking care of business today and see if we can't do the same tomorrow."

His players were used to fielding questions about their coach and the possibility of his return to the NFL. Those questions never ruffled or unsettled them. And during Rose Bowl week, it was more of the same.

"Every single year I've been here, that's always been a rumor," Keegan said. "Obviously, there's been the NFL stuff up in the air and stuff like that, but we know he wants to win a national championship, and that's all that matters right now."

The NFL questions followed him into the next week after the Wolverines arrived in Houston for the national championship game. "I have no idea about that," Harbaugh said at media day. "I couldn't be more happy to be here. This is a tremendous city. They do everything big in Texas, and this is cool. This is right where we want to be." Even when pressed, Harbaugh found a way to answer without saying much. "Yeah, there's a calendar," he said. "I'll gladly talk about the future next week."

While there was so much focus on Harbaugh and a potential jump to the NFL, Yee was also working to negotiate with Michigan and had made progress with Ono, the University of Michigan president who, like Manuel, said all along their goal was to keep Harbaugh in Ann Arbor.

There were sticking points with Michigan, however. While Michigan was prepared to make Harbaugh the highest-paid coach in college football, he wanted assurances regarding the university's response to whatever would come from the two NCAA investigations. He essentially wanted immunity from termination, and he also wanted a three-person arbitration committee as further insurance, so that one person, the athletics director, could not have sole power to fire him.

After the team celebrated the national championship five days after winning it with a parade in the afternoon and an event at the Crisler Center that night, Harbaugh's schedule at Michigan was cleared the following week. He interviewed with the Chargers on January 15 and the next day interviewed with Atlanta. The following week, he flew to Los Angeles the night of January 23 to avoid the icy winter weather that was in the southeast Michigan forecast and to be with the Chargers for a second interview the next day.

Harbaugh was scheduled for a second interview in Atlanta on January 25, so the Chargers knew they had to get the deal done with Harbaugh. On the same afternoon that Harbaugh was meeting with the Chargers, the University of Michigan, after several months of rejecting contract terms his lawyers had proposed, finally came through with a lucrative contract offer that included all the assurances Harbaugh wanted, particularly those regarding the potential outcomes of the two NCAA investigations. Members of his legal team said it was simply too late. Those with knowledge of the contract negotiations from Michigan's side, however, painted a different picture, suggesting it was not a too-little, too-late situation but that Harbaugh had already made up his mind that he was leaving Michigan.

The man who had led Michigan to an 89–25 record, including 40–3 the final three seasons, with three straight wins over Ohio State, three straight Big Ten championships, three straight appearances in the College Football Playoff, and one national championship, had decided to move on to try to win a Super Bowl.

He had been so close to claiming the ultimate prize in football, and that had always nagged at him. While coaching the 49ers from 2011 to 2014, Harbaugh led them to three NFC Championship Games and a Super Bowl after the 2012 season. He lost Super Bowl XLVII to his older brother, John Harbaugh, head coach of the Baltimore Ravens, 34–31, despite San Francisco outscoring them 25–13 in the second half.

For someone as competitive as Harbaugh, losing the Super Bowl was crushing. And while he loves his older brother, John, and the two are close, losing to him stung. In 2015, during a high school coaching clinic Harbaugh hosted at Michigan, he invited John to be the keynote speaker. John took the opportunity to share a story about the postgame greeting with Jim.

John went in for a handshake and had his left arm extended for a hug. Jim stuck his forearm in John's chest and looked him in the eye.

"There will be no hug," Jim said flatly.

John was taken aback.

"There will be no hug," Jim said again before finally uttering congratulations.

At that point, John shrugged, laughed, and told his brother he loved him.

Winning a national championship at Michigan leveled the playing field in a sense in the Harbaugh family. In the postgame news conference, Harbaugh joked he could now sit at the "big person's table in the family." He mentioned that his father, Jack, had won a national championship at Western Kentucky in what was then known as Division I-AA, in addition to his brother winning the Super Bowl.

What this head-coaching job with the Chargers gives him is the knowledge he'll be the only one at that big person's table with the opportunity to have both major football titles—a national championship and a Super Bowl.

Harbaugh left Los Angeles on the night of January 25 after accepting the Chargers job, from Orange County on a Delta flight to Detroit. He apparently had insisted on flying commercial. Harbaugh looked exhausted when he stepped into the terminal from the flight, and he also looked different. The omnipresent dark blue hat with the skinny Block M was not atop his head. In fact, he wasn't wearing any Michigan gear. Under his wind breaker, he wore a powder blue sweater with a sunshine gold Los Angeles Chargers lightning bolt logo on the left side over a powder blue and yellow plaid dress shirt. In a clear bag under his left arm, he carried Chargers gear for his kids.

He walked and talked for about 15 minutes and shared that he would have his final team meeting with the Michigan players the next day. "It's not goodbye," Harbaugh said for a story in the *Detroit News*. "Goodbye is not even a word that resonates." The decision to leave Michigan was "tough," he said, adding in a way only Harbaugh would describe it, that he "tackled it, wrestled it to the ground," while discussing the move with his wife, Sarah, and kids.

"Coaching here has been the love of my life outside of the family," Harbaugh said. "Just our team, everything we did, everything they did, everything the players did, the coaches, the staff. To go from pillar to post and be successful, forever proud to be a part of that. And [at the Chargers], I was there in the building, people were still there who were there when I was still playing [1999–2000]. They were good to me then, they're good to me now, and good to me through the years. Just felt like they left the light on for me."

Having a chance to win a Super Bowl was "one thing" in his decision-making process. It was also about timing and fit. Every time he made a big decision in his coaching career, Harbaugh said there's always been a deep, emotional connection, something that's pulled him in. It started at the University of San Diego, where his head-coaching career was launched.

"How I got to USD in the first place, I was playing for the Chargers, and Monsignor Dan Dillabough was our team priest," Harbaugh said. "We became friends, and he took me over to a USD basketball game in 2000, and we're going to the game, and I was like, 'What's this? This football stadium is beautiful. I love this. I didn't know you guys have got a team.' I just stared at it and said, 'I'm getting into coaching after I get done playing. If you all ever need a coach here, give me a call, please.' He was a trustee there and he called me when I was at the Raiders, so I went there and coached. Then Stanford called—I went to high school there, my dad was defensive coordinator there—and then the 49ers right down the road. And then when I left there, Michigan."

Harbaugh didn't have to spell out his connection to Michigan.

"I'll always be a loyal Wolverine," Harbaugh said.

That he left Michigan with the two unresolved NCAA investigations was not lost on anyone watching his departure from Michigan for Los Angeles. The allegations, the outside noise, never, he said, wore on him.

"Nah, never did," he said. "I can account for myself, and I can account for the players that they were always innocent, and I was innocent. You walk strong and tall and innocent. Didn't mind the priceless motivation. Didn't hurt."

There were other layers to his departure, too. Did Michigan try hard enough to keep him? Did Michigan try hard enough, fast enough? Harbaugh has always maintained a tight circle of confidants making it difficult to get a read on his thinking and decision-making. There were leaks, of course, there always are. There were stories, citing sources, that Michigan made him an offer of a 10-year, $125 million deal. This wasn't true. There was a proliferation of reports that Harbaugh needed to "feel the love" from Michigan and that he and Manuel were at odds.

In the end, he laughed at the rumors and sourced reports and said he knew he was wanted at Michigan and that no one was conspiring against him. He then mentioned a sixth-grade English teacher of his who introduced the concept of critical reading. His point—you can't believe everything you read or, for that matter, hear. As he moved on to the next step of his coaching career, Harbaugh didn't want to point fingers.

"There is no villain," he said. "I've long thought this that when a coach leaves, the only way everybody's happy is if that coach dies. They're either mad at him for leaving, or he's mad at them for firing him. Glad I've got a future. Glad I'm alive."

A few fans stopped Harbaugh along the way for a selfie. They congratulated him on the national championship, and they wished him well on his next coaching endeavor. Harbaugh smiled before he turned to make his way out of the airport.

"I've got one word: gratitude," he said. "That's my word."

And with that, Harbaugh closed the chapter on his Michigan career with gratitude for the successes he enjoyed with his teams and was now looking forward to his next coaching step.

One thing Harbaugh also did upon his return to Detroit after taking the Chargers job was endorse Sherrone Moore as his pick to succeed him at Michigan as head coach. Had Harbaugh returned to coach a 10th season, Moore's contract was expected to be revised to indicate he would be the head coach in waiting. During the summer before the season, Harbaugh, speaking to reporters at a camp held at Wayne State in Detroit for high school prospects, shared that he believed there were at least four assistants on his staff prepared to become head coaches.

Moore clearly was one of them. And in his four-game audition during the 2023 season, with the wins against Bowling Green, and then back-to-back road games against Penn State and Maryland before returning home to lead Michigan to a third-straight win against Ohio State to clinch the Big Ten East Division and a spot in the Big Ten title game, Moore seemed to win over everyone.

"Not a better man to coach the team than Sherrone Moore," Harbaugh said. "I feel like it's in great hands."

Moore, who arrived at Michigan in 2018 from Central Michigan to coach tight ends, had been elevated to heir apparent. In the end, Manuel considered some other coaches to replace Harbaugh, but he only interviewed one, saying he didn't want to "string along" others. Harbaugh became the Chargers head coach on Wednesday; Moore interviewed with Manuel on Thursday; and on Friday, he was named Michigan's 21st head coach. For Manuel, it was that Penn State game on November 11, when it crystallized for him that he might have his next head coach if Harbaugh ever left. Manuel got the call near the team's locker room at Beaver Stadium about 90 minutes before kickoff. The judge said there would be no hearing for the temporary restraining order to attempt to keep Harbaugh on the sideline. The Big Ten's three-game suspension of Harbaugh would stand. He went to speak to Moore, who was on the field.

"He had a look in his eye, and he shook his head and he said, 'Yes, sir, I'll do it,'" Manuel said not long after Moore's introduction as head coach. "He didn't flinch. He was willing to do whatever I thought, Jim thought was best for the team, and he just didn't flinch. Loved it. He is a former offensive lineman, I'm a former defensive lineman, so there's not much that scares us. And I saw that in who he was, and in his eyes, and his reaction to it."

As Manuel watched Michigan run the ball 32 straight times in the second half (the one attempted pass play was negated by a penalty) of the Wolverines' 24–15 victory, he was reminded of his old ball coach at Michigan, Bo Schembechler. "Three yards and a cloud of dust" was how this would have been described back then, but Moore and his offense prefer his more updated description of "smash" football.

After the game, Manuel called Harbaugh and said that, undoubtedly, Moore was the right coach to lead the team on game days in his absence. After all, Harbaugh was able to still coach practices and have game-plan input during the week.

"To be told 90 minutes before a game [that] you're taking over against a team like Penn State in an environment like Penn State, and to see his poise and the way he handled things, both leading the team, calling the plays, making the decisions, that was the time, when after talking to Jim about him, I realized that this could be our next head coach," Manuel said. "At some point. Obviously, I didn't realize it would be at the end of this season. This is really six years of a process to get to know him. It wasn't just the Penn State game, but that was the culmination, for lack of a better word, of knowing he's ready."

Looking back, no one could have been surprised that Moore's four games as acting head coach were, ultimately, an audition. As Manuel would say, no one planned on that. But Moore, he said, "aced" it.

During his four games as acting head coach in 2023, Moore had to balance coaching the offensive line, calling the plays while being the head coach (a role, he said, that required him to move out of his comfort zone), as well as spending more time talking to the officials. "Doing it and doing it in a big game, there was a good bit [of balancing]," Moore said of all the hats he wore those four games. "I wouldn't say it was too much."

Moore said at his formal introductory news conference that he had prepared his entire coaching career for this moment, to take over a major program. The 37-year-old Moore, an offensive lineman at Oklahoma, had been building toward this since beginning his coaching career with Louisville as a graduate assistant from 2009 to 2011. He was then promoted to tight ends coach through 2013, before moving to Central Michigan as tight ends coach from 2014 to 2016. In 2017, he was promoted to the Chippewas' assistant head coach, continued to coach tight ends, and also became recruiting coordinator.

But then he made a pivotal career shift and joined Harbaugh's staff the following year.

"I got a recommendation—'He's a really good coach at Central Michigan,'" Harbaugh told reporters before the national championship game. "'He's coaching the tight ends. His name is Sherrone Moore. You should at least bring him in and talk to him.' I called him on the phone. I said, 'Sherrone, this is Coach Harbaugh, can you come over to Ann Arbor, I want to talk to you about the tight ends job here at Michigan.'"

Moore was in Harbaugh's office the next day.

"The first time we sit down, we meet each other, and then I asked him, 'Just show me your technique of a zone block and a gap block for a tight end,'" Harbaugh said. "He jumped up and just started demonstrating and went through this teaching progression that was, *boom*, one, two, three, four, and memorable, learnable. First time I met him, I was blown away. He knocked my socks off."

Moore joined Harbaugh's staff as tight ends coach in 2018 and quickly moved up the ladder. By 2021, he was co–offensive coordinator and offensive-line coach and stayed in those roles in 2022. Moore led Michigan's offensive lines to back-to-back Joe Moore Awards as the nation's top offensive line. In 2023, he was elevated to offensive coordinator and became the primary play-caller while coaching the offensive line for a third season. Little did he or anyone know, he would lead Michigan to four wins as acting head coach.

What fans saw in those wins from Moore's coaching is what Harbaugh said he knew all along. "You've already got a glimpse of the shining star that he is," Harbaugh said. "He's just phenomenal, so smart, works so hard at it. He knows what it's like to be a player. He was a player. And he's really, really composed. Something goes wrong—three, two, one—let it go. He's tremendous at that.

"He was never better than he was in that two-minute drive in the Rose Bowl and in overtime. Knew he had to call the game, the drive of his life, and he did. We saw the same thing when he's coaching against Ohio State in the Big House. The same thing when he went to Penn State. How about that? You've got to go to Penn State, you find out the day before the game, in addition to your offensive-line coaching duties, your offensive-coordinating play duties, and your play-calling duties, you're also going to make the head coach decisions as well. Sherrone Moore, shining star. No doubt about it."

Moore said his focus for the players and coaches will be three key phases that will be the foundation of his new role as head coach: process, pursuit, and standard.

"We continue to talk about the process over the prize, and the prize we've got," Moore said. "But we're hungry for more. Now we're in the pursuit, the pursuit of greatness, and to do that, you gotta push, you gotta strain, you gotta do that every single day on and off the field to be great. And that will take you to the standard. And once we continue to win on and off the field, we will become the standard. And that's the goal here at the University of Michigan, and nothing less."

Moore's hiring as head coach also made history at Michigan, as he became the program's first Black head football coach. Manuel, who also is Black, said he understood how impactful it was to hire a Black head coach, but assured that was not what influenced his decision. "It had no bearing, but I understand the magnitude of choosing him," Manuel said. "Look, this institution is 207 years old. And 145 years [of Michigan football], and it's the first Black man to take the reins. As someone who understands history, I feel great about it because he's ready. And the fact that he's Black, it really sends a message that there are opportunities that can be had. There's not a lot of Black coaches in Power 5 institutions. I take a lot of pride in that. If you heard my statement and you heard Sherrone's statement, the reason I kept it out, is because I didn't want anyone to even think that that had anything to do with this decision."

Moore considers it an honor becoming Michigan's first Black head football coach, calling it a privilege and not something he takes lightly.

"For all the African American men that have worked, I just want to show them that you can do it regardless of being African American, being white, I want to show if you're a good coach, if you work your tail off, that dreams can come true," Moore said. "And I want to be an inspiration to people that have that vision that want to do that. It means a lot. I take a lot of pride in that and continue to do that."

Edwards, the Michigan running back, attended Moore's introductory news conference in a show of support for his new head coach and called it an honor seeing Moore as the program's first Black head coach.

"He truly deserves it," Edwards said. "I'm just star-struck because this is never about who is what. Him as a man, him as a leader, he just deserves to be the head coach. Couldn't be any more proud of him to be a head coach. He's worked his butt off to be in the position he's in. He deserves it. He deserves the opportunity."

Manuel said wanting to make history at Michigan by hiring a Black head football coach was not a motivation and never entered the process. He and Moore, during the interview, never even brought up what his hiring would mean on that level.

"But am I proud of him for being the first Black head coach? Absolutely," Manuel said. "But I didn't look at him and say, 'Yeah, I got an opportunity to hire the first Black head coach.' I didn't even think about it that way, because in the interview, it was about him coaching, and what he's gonna do and how he's gonna handle everything and do everything. Didn't come up in the interview process.

"We talked about the magnitude of it [later]. I'm happy for him, happy for the university. It's what Michigan is about, regardless of the color of your skin, pairing the best person for the job and moving things forward. And I take a lot of pride that he's the best man for the job. And the fact that he's Black makes me feel good as a Black person, Black male, that he's developed to that level where he can take over this program."

Now it's his time to flex his coaching muscles as the leader of the Michigan football team. He understands what Harbaugh meant to the program, leading it the last three seasons to three straight Big Ten titles, College Football Playoff appearances, and the national championship. And he also knows it can be a challenge to be the leader who follows an established coach.

"I'm just gonna be me. I can't be a Coach [Harbaugh]," Moore said. "I love Coach, Coach loves this university. I've watched him coach for the last six years, but I can't be Jim Harbaugh. So I'm going to be me, and I think in this business and in any world, if you're not yourself, you're gonna lose the people around you. So I'm definitely going to be myself, be who I am. My leadership style is how I'm going to approach things and do that. I'm definitely gonna lean on him tremendously because obviously what we've built here, but definitely going to just be myself."

Moore said his leadership style is evolving,

"You'll see that over time," Moore said. "My No. 1 philosophy is I coach hard, but I love harder. I'm going to coach these kids extremely hard. The guys that have been in my [offensive-line] room know that. They know I'm gonna coach 'em hard, but that I'm going to love 'em. And at the end of the day, they know that I'm gonna do everything in the best interest of them and for this team."

And with that, the torch had been passed.

ACKNOWLEDGMENTS

MANY THANKS to Triumph Books, particularly Bill Ames, for giving me the opportunity to write this book. Editor Alex Lubertozzi was exceptional to work with, thorough and patient.

Thank you to the *Detroit News* for allowing me to take on this project. Special thanks to sports editor Rod Beard and assistant sports editor Daren Tomhave, two of the very best people I know. I am so appreciative of my colleagues, columnists John Niyo and Bob Wojnowski. They are real pros and terrific writers. Tony Paul is an important *Detroit News* teammate and MVP of this staff, who is always there for an assist and to answer my many phone calls. I'd be remiss if I didn't tip the hat to former sports editors Phil Laciura, who hired me, and Jim Russ.

The Michigan alumni fan base is exceptionally large, and I've become close to a few. I am delighted to call Eric Champnella a friend and appreciate his humor and our shared love of tennis. It was great seeing him enjoy the national championship game with his son, Derek. Also, a special shout-out to Randy Winograd, who has been so generous with his time and friendship. And to Tyler Patterson, my brilliant friend. I am grateful you share your insights with me.

Michigan football also brought my dear friend Andrea Agathoklis Murino into my life, thanks to her husband and Michigan alum John

Murino. She is truly a gift. I also gained a wonderful friend in Ashley Bastock, who worked the Michigan beat for the *Toledo Blade*. She is now with Cleveland.com covering the Browns, and I love watching her career continue to grow.

Many thanks to Meredith Weaver for carrying me in golf all those years and for being such a great, constant friend. Your support means so much. The Greek church is very important to me, and I am thankful for my friendship with Andrea Feles-Katsimbaris and her husband, Yianni. Also, a special shout-out to the ladies of Philoptochos.

And thank you to my family. My mother Cleopatra is always an inspiration, and she never ceases to entertain me with her college football knowledge and questions. I could not have better or more supportive siblings than Stephanie, Gregory, and Stratin. They have been all great role models for me. Lastly, I think about my late father William every day, and he is missed.